MW00753499

LD 4511196 0

Pearl Lowe's
VINTAGE CRAFT

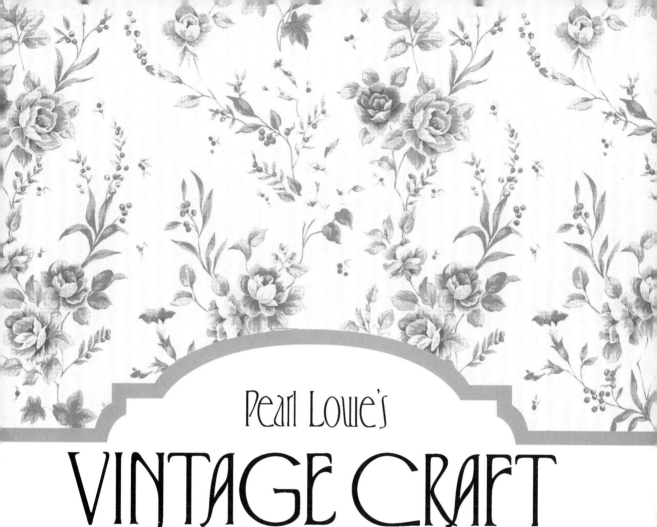

Pearl Lowe's
VINTAGE CRAFT

Craft projects & styling advice
for the modern vintage home

Contents

Welcome to my Vintage Home

As a child I always wanted to be different from everyone around me and to be able to express my own personal style. I chose the clothes I liked and drove my mother mad by insisting on only wearing clothes that were unique, and if anyone bought something I had, I never wore it again! Vintage clothing made copying my style very difficult – I had no fear of ever bumping into anyone wearing the same thing as me.

Getting into vintage styling was a natural thing for me, but it wasn't my first vocation. I started my career as a singer, which was all I ever wanted to do as a child, but when I had children and the singing and touring came to an end, I decided I had to find something else to do. At the time, I'd just bought my first renovation house, in Camden, London. It was a wreck and I didn't have much money, so I decorated it simply by painting all the walls and floors white and punctuating the whole look with dashes of colour throughout the rooms. I even did this in the bathroom, by putting up a lace curtain I had dyed a fuchsia colour. It was this curtain that started my career as a designer: a neighbour saw it and showed it to a friend who owned a lifestyle boutique in Notting Hill. They loved it and asked if they could stock my curtains. They sold out almost instantly, but not before the editor of *Elle Decoration* noticed the curtains and asked me for a bright red version. She then commissioned a ten-page article on my vintage style and everything snowballed from there.

It's the history and style of days gone by that excite and inspire me when I'm designing for my home or for a collection. My favourite periods are the 1920s and 1950s; they were eras of glamour and romance, of beautiful people, beautiful clothes and beautiful furniture, and I believe we are all entitled to a little bit of glamour in our lives – and glamour never goes out of fashion. Because period items become rarer over the years – they become damaged or are discarded and lost – they can come with an expensive price tag in some of the boutique shops, but don't let that hold you back; you just need to get savvy and know where to hunt for the bargains.

I particularly enjoy trawling around flea markets, vintage fairs, car boot sales and online, hunting out genuine vintage pieces, but because they are old they can be difficult to find in good condition. The good news is that this style can be easily and inexpensively mimicked, so you don't have to go vintage – you can go vintage-style and it doesn't matter! That's the beauty of this look: you can create the detail yourself or with a little help from a specialist craftsman.

If you don't mind a bit of damage, then the choice of original pieces is even greater – everything doesn't have to look perfect. In fact, I think flaws add character. For instance, I love roll-top baths (I get them cheap on eBay) and I don't mind it when they have a few chips in the enamel as I think it gives them soul and history.

Use your imagination when you're out hunting for bargains; if you see something that's a bit chipped or marked, think what you (or some other crafty person) can do to get it looking the way you want it to. Slightly damaged

pieces can be given a new lease of life with a bit of imagination: dressers and armoires can be painted; damaged door panels can be replaced with glass, wire grilles or lace; lampshades can be dressed up with lace or fringing; and sagging sofas can be reupholstered in your favourite fabric. As long as the piece you buy is pretty much fit for purpose and not irreparable, you can make it whatever you wish.

I do upcycle objects and decorate many things myself, but I know my limitations and also when I need to I call in an expert to help me create something really beautiful. Carpenters, furniture restorers and electricians will become your best friends as you ask for their expertise in revamping old or new pieces, but there are also great crafters around who can help if you are not so handy with a needle or a paintbrush. There's a wonderful lady in Bath, for example, who makes all my pretty padded clothes hangers for me.

It's these people who have inspired this book. With their help I have managed to turn many of my homes over the years into my vintage dream. I have moved roughly every two years, always looking for the next project, and so I've picked up lots of tips along the way, which I want to share with you here. I hope this book will inspire you to create your ideal home; alongside all the advice I've found useful over the years, I've included plenty of ideas and practical projects to show you how easy it can be to upcycle furniture and other objects to create beautiful vintage-style pieces. From painted tiles, homemade cakestands and my signature dyed lace, to headboards for beds, painted chests and découpage chairs, there are loads of suggestions for how you can inexpensively create the look. In between the projects, I've shared with you how I go about styling rooms and how I like to create the look using both vintage and vintage-style pieces – I've also spilled the beans as to where I get my best bits from (the secret is out!).

Vintage styling isn't about clutter and lots and lots of mismatched pieces (although that works too, sometimes); it's about choosing things that work well together and complement each other. What I love about it is that it's a really personal style, and one that reflects your personality. You don't have to follow all these craft projects to the letter,

they are here to inspire you to create your own look – change the colours or the patterns to make them your own, mix and match objects wherever you want, vamp it up or tone it down. Be brave to make things beautiful, go with your instinct and passion and you will create your own unique and stylish home, and have a lot of fun in the process.

Nº1

Heavenly Kitchen
&
Picture Perfect
Dining

A pretty stand can make even the most humble shop-bought pastry something worthy of a Parisian patisserie, so here's my guide to making one of your very own. Don't feel limited to three plates for your stand – use four or five if you like.

Tiered cake stand

you will need

3 plates
Water-soluble marker
Safety glasses
Cordless drill with a tile drill-bit
Three-tier cake-stand fitting, which comes with rods, screws and washers
Screwdriver

1 Select the plates you wish to use. You will need a dinner plate for the bottom, a side plate for the middle and a saucer for the top. For an Alice-in-Wonderland feel, use a china cup for the final tier. Mismatched patterns work really well, but try to tie the plates together in some way – whether through a theme, such as birds or a pretty floral motif, or a complementary design or colour scheme.

2 Make sure your plates are clean and dry and without cracks. Very occasionally, if a plate has a hairline crack or is especially delicate, it will break when you drill it. Measure the diameter of each plate and mark the middle of each with a water-soluble marker. This will act as your drill guide.

3 Put on your safety glasses and, on a safe and secure surface, such as a workbench or well-protected table, slowly drill where you have marked the middle of each plate until you have passed all the way through. It's worth noting that the glaze on some vintage plates makes them impossible to drill through, which you won't know about until you start trying to drill. In this case, unfortunately you'll have to find another plate.

4 Assemble the cake stand following the manufacturer's instructions for the fittings.

PEARLS *of* WISDOM

As an alternative to the cake-stand fitting, you could also try egg cups or small glasses or goblets as the risers between each plate. Glue them into place using a hot glue gun.

Bohemian
herb planters

I love using unusual containers for a delicious display of those ever-useful herbs such as basil, coriander and sage, together with something more decorative, like lavender. It's all about creating an enchanting display at different heights and levels.

you will need

Cut-glass dessert dishes and other vintage glassware and crockery
Herbs from a garden centre
Small bag of potting compost
A4 sheet of thick card, and a pen
Wooden stirrers
Hot glue gun

1 To pot your herbs, half-fill the cut-glass dishes with the compost. Gently ease the herbs from their small pots and place them on the compost. When planting herbs, always consider the size of the plant that you are potting compared to the container. If you are using plug plants, you may find you can fit in two or three per dish.

2 Add small handfuls of the compost around the herbs, gently pressing it firm, until the dish is almost full. It is best not to fill the pot right to the top because when the compost is watered it will swell slightly.

3 Stand your plants on a light windowsill but not in direct sunlight, and water them regularly.

4 To label your herbs, cut small labels from the thick card and write the herb names on them. Then use the hot glue gun to attach them firmly to the wooden stirrers. Push them into the compost alongside each herb.

Painting glass Kilner jars is a quick and simple way to add a touch of vintage to your everyday kitchen items. You can also decorate jam jars, milk bottles or any glass containers you care to lay your paintbrush on. A perfect solution for storing dry goods and kitchen utensils, they also make great gifts when filled with sweets and tied with a ribbon.

Glass-painted Kilner jars

you will need

Stencil outline (see page 224)
Cutting mat
A4 sheet of transparent acetate
Masking tape
Craft knife
Kilner jars
Glass paints in a variety of colours
Stippling brush

1 If you are using a design from this book, photocopy it (enlarging if necessary). If you are making your own design, simply draw it on some paper. Lay the design on the cutting mat and then lay the acetate over the top and secure it in place with some masking tape.

2 Using a sharp craft knife, begin cutting along the longest, straightest edges of the stencil design, as these are the easiest. Try to cut each line only once, so make sure you press firmly and smoothly. Use your free hand to secure the acetate and image, but make sure you keep your fingers well away from where you are cutting. As you are cutting, turn the cutting mat so you are always cutting at an easy angle and away from you as much as possible.

3 Once you have cut out the whole design, tidy up any rough edges (so paint doesn't get caught up in these), and your stencil is ready to use.

4 Attach the stencil to a jar with the masking tape and then, on a prepared work surface, apply paint using the stippling brush. Load the brush with some paint, but not too much, and use a gentle stabbing motion to apply the paint through the stencil. Leave the jar to dry overnight, carefully remove the stencil and fill with whatever you fancy. Always wash by hand.

PEARLS of WISDOM

These jars are great for storage, but they are equally pretty with a tea light inside or some fresh flowers standing in them. The jars in the photograph feature a stencilled design, and also some roses that have been painted freehand. Unleash your creativity and experiment!

I always enjoy trawling old tile shops and reclamation yards looking for pretty and unique designs to refresh a sink splashback or a plain bathroom scheme. But, if you can't find what you want, make your own! I recommend trying one tile before considering decorating your entire bathroom. Here are two simple methods.

Handmade vintage-style tiles

Decorating with transfers

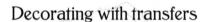

you will need

Royalty- or copyright-free image, or a design of your own to fit the tiles

A4 inkjet waterslide transfer paper

Inkjet printer (it must be inkjet; this process isn't compatible with a laserjet printer)

Plain tiles, avoiding any with a glazed, rough or textured surface

D-cut squeegee

Sponge

1 Select your image and print it onto the waterslide transfer paper using an inkjet printer and following the manufacturer's instructions. Remember that the image will ultimately be reversed, so don't choose a picture that will look odd when it's back to front – for example, images that contain words or numbers. If you are creating your own design, you will need to scan it in to your computer first.

2 Put the printed design into a bowl or sink full of warm water and wait for 60 seconds until the design can be removed from the backing paper.

3 On a prepared work surface, slip the design from the backing paper onto the surface of a clean and dry tile and use the squeegee to make it smooth. Wash away any gum from the surface of the design with a clean damp sponge. Leave the tile to dry at room temperature for 8–10 hours.

4 Preheat the oven to 140°C (275°F/Gas mark 1), then put the tile in the oven for 10–20 minutes to seal the transfer. You will know it is ready when the image turns shiny, as if glazed. Turn off the oven and let the tile cool down before taking it out and putting it to one side to cool completely at room temperature. It is now ready for tiling. Always wash decorated tiles by hand in warm soapy water.

Handmade vintage-style tiles

Decorating with ceramic pens

you will need

Plain tiles, avoiding any with a glazed, rough or textured surface
High-gloss water-based ceramic pens
Stencils (see page 224) (optional)
A4 sheet of acetate (optional)
Ceramic varnish (optional)

1 If you are a confident artist, you can draw your design directly onto the tiles with the water-based ceramic pens. Alternatively, make a stencil of your design using the acetate (see page 17) and use this for drawing onto the tiles. Set the tiles to one side for at least 4 hours until the paint has dried.

2 Preheat the oven to 170°C (375°F/Gas mark 5), then put the tiles in the oven for 25–30 minutes until they are touch-dry. Turn off the oven and let the tiles cool down before taking them out and putting to one side to cool completely at room temperature. If you wish, you can seal the tiles once they are cool with ceramic varnish. They are now ready for tiling. Always wash tiles by hand in warm soapy water.

Découpage chair

Brighten up an old kitchen chair or dining table with a coat of paint and découpage. The options are as endless as your imagination; you could go for a unified colour scheme and a single subtle motif or a range of colours and bold layered découpage – whatever works in your home. This is also a fantastic way to upcycle a tired wooden desk chair or other wooden furniture.

you will need

Dust sheet or newspaper
Sandpaper in various grades and your choice of paint (see page 210)
Wooden chair
Printed royalty- or copyright-free image
Découpage glue

1 Protect your work area with a dust sheet or newspaper and prepare and paint the chair (see page 210).

2 Stick the printed image onto the chair with the découpage glue. Paint over the image with a layer of the découpage glue, which dries to a clear seal. Let the chair dry for at least 5 hours.

Hippy Gypsy

I think I've always been a bit of a gypsy at heart. I've been reading tarots for people since I was 13 years old and I'm always on the move; I seem to get restless after being in a house for about 18 months, especially once I've got it just as I like it. My eldest son Alfie recently worked out that he has moved 14 times in his life – and he's only 15!

So it's no surprise that I feel very much at home with the whole hippy gypsy style, not least because it also echoes the Stevie Nicks look that started off my love of vintage style – lots of black lace and shawls and plenty of vibrantly-coloured cushions.

Five years ago I got my chance to really embrace the gypsy style when I found a pretty 1950s cream caravan on eBay for £250. Over the next couple of months I painted the outside mint green, then inside I covered the walls in a black floral Ralph Lauren wallpaper, the beds in black velvet, the windows with black lace curtains, and accessorised with lace and silk cushions. I even put up an old chandelier that I found in an antique shop in Islington.

It was just stunning, and it became my little haven; I spent hours reading and writing in it when the kids were at school. It looked so lovely that it even made it into *Vogue* magazine. When we then moved to a townhouse we had to sell it as we had nowhere to store it, but when we moved back to the country, I decided to look for another one. I gave an interview where I said that I was looking for a gypsy wagon to renovate, and someone tweeted me to say that their parents had one in a village that was literally just ten minutes away. It had been in the family for more than 70 years and it was charming. I loved it at once and my husband Danny bought it for my birthday present – what a fantastic gift!

I spent hours looking for inspiration for decorating the gypsy wagon. I really admire interior designer Sera Loftus's style, who has the gypsy look down to perfection, and I have also recently come across fashion and interiors brand Magnolia Pearl; they own the most wonderful Airstream that has been revamped into a gypsy haven. Inspired, I then got cracking on the renovation. My local builder gutted the caravan and made wooden slats for a bed. I then lined the ceiling in Kate Forman fabric and covered a large mattress with a vintage patchwork quilt and vintage fur throw, and added lots of velvet and tapestry cushions. For the exterior, I called a local artist called Faye Chadburn and showed her some sketches of the sort of flowers and butterflies that I wanted painted on the outside – they weren't traditional gypsy stencils because I wanted it to be completely original. The finished effect is magical and exactly what I hoped it would be.

eBay has lots of caravans for sale, but obviously the older and rarer 1920s, 1930s or 1940s wagons are much more expensive. Real Romany wagons, depending on their age and condition, can cost even more.

Of course, you can really go to town in a caravan, but you don't have to have one to enjoy the hippy gypsy look; it can easily be recreated anywhere in the house, although it works best in small rooms or corners of rooms if you want to get that really cosy feel.

This look is essentially about layering – lots of floral prints on the walls or as soft furnishings, embellished with accessories made from crocheted lace and strongly textured fabrics. Think rich, primal colours, such as reds and yellows, and lots of sumptuous, exotic fabrics. Indian sari materials and exquisite silks are perfect, as are tapestry cushions and crushed velvet in deep jewel-like shades. With this look you need more – more cushions and more bedspreads – all piled up to create a luxurious, intimate atmosphere. Keep the cosy feel going with low-level lighting. I love chandeliers, and in this case antique ones with hanging crystals to reflect the light are a match made in heaven, but if you have space, you can scatter candles in Moroccan or gold-leafed tea-light holders around the room. Enhance this Bedouin tent-like look by hanging lace or silks from the ceiling over a bed or simply over large cushions on the floor. If you can find them, Moroccan or Middle-Eastern quilts and hangings look fabulously authentic.

The joy of this look is that you can use it anywhere. It is heaven in an adult's bedroom; you can tone it down with finer lace for a child's bedroom; you can use it in a sitting room or the corner of a playroom – or you can even take it outside and, on a warm summer's day or evening, create your own exotic holiday destination in your back garden.

Being practical yet a little stylish in the kitchen is important to me, as very often I am still wearing my apron when guests arrive. This simple pinny design was inspired by a gypsy skirt and uses rich colours and floral patterns. A sewing machine isn't essential, but it is preferable. Similarly, a tailor's dummy would be helpful or, failing that, a willing volunteer.

Gypsy-style apron

you will need

44 x 78cm (17½ x 31in) fabric for the main skirt section
130 x 20cm (51 x 8in) fabric for the frilly hem
180 x 5cm (71 x 2in) wide ribbon for the tie
30 x 30cm (12 x 12in) fabric for the pocket
1m x 2cm (1yd x ¾in) lace or braid
2 tassels (optional)
Sewing machine (optional)

1 On each edge of the main skirt fabric, press a 5mm (¼in) hem to the wrong side and then fold again by 1.5cm (in). Press again, then pin and stitch. On the top edge of the skirt, press 1.5cm (in) to the front. Pin, but don't stitch.

2 To give the top of the skirt some shape, make five 1cm (½in) pleats at each end. Starting 5cm (2in) from one end, fold the fabric in on itself by 1cm (½in). Pin in place. Repeat four more times with each pleat about 2.5cm (1in) apart. Repeat at the other end of the top of the skirt. Stitch in place with a running stitch (see page 208) or using a sewing machine, about 1cm (½in) from the edge. Remove the pins.

3 For the frill for the bottom, press in 1cm (½in) along the long edge that will be the top of the frill and stitch in place with loose running stitches. With the loose piece of thread at one end, gently pull it to make gathers. Pull up

until the frill is the same length along the top edge as the bottom of the main fabric (about 78cm/31in). Secure the thread by wrapping it around a pin inserted into the frill.

4 Pin the frill to the bottom of the skirt so that the right side of the frill is overlapping the right side of the main fabric by about 2cm (¾in), and with a small amount at each end wrapping round onto the back. Stitch in place and remove the pins.

5 For the tie, pin the ribbon to the right side of the skirt at the top, aligning the top edge of the ribbon with the top of the skirt. Stitch along both sides of the ribbon and also across the ribbon at each side of the main fabric. At the ends of the ribbon, fold over the edges towards the wrong side to make a point. Stitch in place.

6 Cut out the pocket to the desired shape and press in 3mm (in) along the top edge and then 5mm (¼in) and stitch in place with slip stitch (see page 208). Then stitch on the lace or braid around the remaining edges. Pin the pocket to the main part of the apron, ensuring it is centred, and then stitch firmly in place.

7 Finish the apron with a tassel at each end of the ribbon tie, if you wish.

I like my kitchen items to have a practical use but also to suit my style. Even the humble tea towel can make a statement when hanging from a door or draped over an oven door handle. Sewing with black embroidery thread gives a modern twist to traditional cross-stitch.

Blackbird cross-stitch tea towel

you will need

56 x 72cm (22 x 28½in) white cotton fabric or plain white tea towel
Sewing machine (optional)
56cm (22in) cotton tassel braid
56cm (22in) lace border
12 x 9cm (4¾ x 3½in) piece of 14-count soluble canvas
15cm (6in) embroidery hoop (optional)
Cotton embroidery thread: black or colour of your choice
Cross-stitch pattern (see page 225)
Towel
Fabric dye (optional)

1 Press in 5mm (¼in) and then 1cm (½in) all the way around the fabric. Stitch in place using slip stitch (see page 208), or use a sewing machine. You could use a plain tea towel instead.

2 Pin the tassel braid to the bottom hem of the tea towel and sew using a running stitch (see page 208) or use a sewing machine.

3 Measure 10cm (4in) from the tassel braid, then pin and sew the lace border using a running stitch.

4 Pin and tack the soluble canvas onto the tea towel where you want the pattern to sit. Here, the pattern starts 5cm (2in) from the left-hand side and roughly 5mm (¼in) from the black lace.

If you are using an embroidery hoop, place it around the soluble canvas and gently pull the fabric taut.

5 Stitch the bird using cross-stitches and following the chart (see page 225). You will only need to stitch with two strands of the thread. To separate them, cut a length of embroidery thread from the skein roughly twice the length of your forearm and gently separate out the strands by running your thumb down the thread, making sure you continue to hold the two groups tightly.

6 When you have finished stitching, remove the hoop and the tacking stitches.

7 Soak the embroidered material in a clean bowl of lukewarm water for around 10 minutes until all the soluble canvas has dissolved and you are just left with your stitches. Leave your tea towel to dry naturally, laid flat on a towel.

8 For an extra finishing touch, hand-dye the tea towel to give it an aged look. Follow the dye manufacturer's instructions.

9 Once dry (or nearly dry), turn your embroidery face down on a towel and iron on the back to ensure that you don't crush your stitches with the iron.

Appliquéd & embroidered rose tea towel

you will need

56 x 72cm (22 x 28½in) white cotton fabric or a plain white tea towel

Sewing machine (optional)

Appliqué template and embroidery design (see page 224)

Tracing paper

Embroidery needle and cotton embroidery thread: pink or colour of your choice

25 x 25cm (10 x 10in) appliqué fabric

1 Press in 5mm (¼in) and then 1cm (½in) all the way around the fabric. Stitch in place using slip stitch (see page 208) or use a sewing machine. You could use a plain tea towel instead.

2 Copy the rose pattern on page 224 onto the tracing paper and then pin it to the fabric where you want the pattern to be positioned. Work small running stitches with a contrasting colour of cotton thread through both layers around all the outlines, then remove the tracing paper.

3 Using six and two strands of the embroidery thread, and working in back stitch, embroider over the running stitches. To separate the threads, cut a length of embroidery thread from the skein roughly twice the length of your forearm and gently separate out the strands by running your thumb down the thread, making sure you continue to hold the two groups tightly.

4 Carefully remove the running stitches using small embroidery scissors.

5 For the appliquéd leaves, trace the pattern of the leaves and the area that covers where the rose has been embroidered onto tracing paper. Pin the paper to the fabric and cut out the shapes, cutting through both the fabric and tracing paper (you can keep the paper if you want to use the pattern again).

6 Pin the appliqué fabric to the tea towel and sew on with cotton or embroidery thread using a neat running stitch. Leave a rough edge to add a rustic touch. You could also use slightly larger leaves (increase the design on a photocopier by roughly 30 per cent) and slip stitch them in place.

PEARLS *of* WISDOM

If you want to add a hanging loop on one corner, stitch on some braid or ribbon. Fasten securely with a running stitch.
You could create you own design for the embroidery or use one of the other motifs from this book (see page 224).

the

Perfect Finish

IS ALL

in the

DETAIL

Entertaining Vintage Style

I love my home and Danny loves to cook. We're both really sociable and can think of nothing better than spending time with friends over a lingering lunch or a decadent dinner. Whether we're eating inside or out, celebrating a special occasion or just casually catching up with friends or family, I like to make a big effort and sit everyone down around a stylishly set table.

No matter how nice your table is as a piece of furniture, it always looks better when dressed. I think every meal deserves a tablecloth – it adds a bit of sophistication – and I prefer mine to create a neutral background so that my vintage accessories can dictate the look. It's hard to find the genuine article as tablecloths from yesteryear were often made from delicate fabrics that have become damaged or simply deteriorated over the years, but there are lots of new vintage-style cloths around; my favourites are linen and crêpe with pretty small floral patterns. I think pastel-coloured cloths look better than white, as they add a bit of colour, but if you do go for white and fancy brightening it up, you can always place a coloured lace runner (see page 41) or a full cloth over the top (and if you don't like the colour of a cheap bit of fabric – dye it to one you do like). Piano shawls with delicate fringing can also look fabulous.

Napkins make a meal special and really show you're making an effort, and I like delicately dyed ones and those with a lace inset that have an air of shabby chic. I prefer napkins to have a similar style to what's on the table, but they don't have to be identical – I have been known to use different colours across the table, either in tones of pastels or bright colours. The Goth in me also enjoys throwing tradition to the wind and laying out a black and red scheme for a dinner party.

When it comes to crockery, I definitely like to mix and match. You can easily get hold of vintage plates quite cheaply in charity shops, car boot sales or flea markets. Buy what you love; it doesn't matter if they are a bit faded or don't go together, that's the joy of the look. If they aren't quite what you dreamed of, you can always get arty and decorate them using enamel or ceramic paints then bake the plates in the oven to seal.

Although I adore the informality of mixed styles of crockery, I do think a table looks better if the glasses have a uniform look, otherwise the scheme can get a bit chaotic. Again, you can get hold of vintage glasses at all the usual places, but it can be hard to get hold of a complete set, or even enough for a large group of friends, so you are probably better off buying such glassware from shops that sell vintage-style homeware.

Whether you are eating during the day or evening, jam jars of freshly picked flowers look gorgeous and really bring the table together. If you've got a good selection in the garden, this can be cheaply and easily done, or you can pick up a bouquet from a florist. I like to include sprigs of rosemary and lavender from the garden in my jars, which fill out the arrangements but also add a wonderful fragrance.

I admit it, I have an obsession with chandeliers, but when we have friends over in the evening it is one of the few times that I leave the lights off. I think a dinner table has more atmosphere with tea lights scattered over it, nestling among flowers with their light sparkling off the jam jars and the pretty glassware. I also have some vintage-style silver candle holders that I light in the evening. It can get a bit gloomy at night if you just stick to candles, so I also like to hang strings of fairy lights around the walls, which softly light the room as we while away the evening.

Entertaining vintage style can be achieved on a really small budget, no matter how sophisticated the look, as long as you think first about how the accessories you buy will work together. Keep it simple and don't over-clutter the table – remember that atmosphere is everything.

This tablecloth is not one for everyday use, but it will make your kitchen table a little bit special. I have used ivory lace and black cotton, but choose fabric and colours that suit your style. The instructions given here make a tablecloth that measures 2.8 x 1.6m (9 x 5ft): it has nine rows, each with five squares.

Patchwork lace tablecloth

you will need

About 2m (2yd) cotton fabric, cut into 23 31cm (12½in) squares

22 pre-cut and hemmed lace squares, each 30cm (12in) square

Sewing machine with overlock function

9m x 11cm (10yd x 4½in) lace border

1 Press under 1cm (½in) on each edge of the cotton squares.

2 Working across one row of squares, right sides up, and alternating lace and fabric, pin five squares together, overlapping by about 5mm (¼in). Stitch together using overlock stitch on the sewing machine.

3 Repeat for the remaining eight rows, but alternate the order of the fabric and lace. Stitch together the rows in the same way to make one large tablecloth.

4 To finish, cut the lace border into four pieces to match the length and width of the tablecloth but with an additional 22cm (9in) on each piece for mitring the corners. With right sides up, pin the fabric over the border with 11cm (4½in) excess at each end. Stitch together using overlock stitch, as before. If your lace border is narrower or wider than 11cm (4½in), you will need to adjust the excess for mitring accordingly.

5 To mitre the corners, pin and tack together the lace border at a 45-degree angle to the corner of the main fabric, with right sides facing. Press the excess fabric to one side and then overlock the layers together, right side uppermost. Trim the excess. Repeat for each corner.

Dressing the table and creating the perfect atmosphere is really important to me, especially for a big occasion. Choose the colours and fabrics you love; I simply adore heritage black lace, and have softened it by layering the beautiful scalloped design with dusky pink satin to create a gothic but feminine feel.

Satin & lace runner and place mats

you will need

For the runner
About 183 x 40cm (72 x 16in) pink satin
About 183 x 40cm (72 x 16in) black lace
Sewing machine (optional)
80cm (32in) black fringe
For each mat
40 x 30cm (16 x 12in) pink satin
40 x 30cm (16 x 12in) black lace

1 Measure the width of the table and divide the measurement by four. This will give you the approximate width of the runner. Then measure the length of the area that you want the runner to cover. Add 3cm (1¼in) to the length and width and cut out the satin and lace to these dimensions. You may want to run it just across the centre of the table or make it longer so that it overhangs at each end. Amend the length accordingly.

2 To make the runner, press in 5mm (¼in) and then 1cm (½in) on each edge of the satin. Stitch in place using slip stitch (see page 208) or use a sewing machine.

3 Lay the lace on your work surface, right side down, and lay the satin on top, also right side down. Pin the excess lace onto the back of the satin and stitch in place, about 1cm (½in) in from the edges.

4 Cut two pieces of the fringe for each end of the runner. Add a little extra to the length for a neat finish. Pin the fringe to the right side of the runner, tucking under the allowance to the wrong side. Stitch in place.

5 For each place mat, press in 5mm (¼in) and then 1cm (½in) on each edge of the satin. Stitch in place using slip stitch or use a sewing machine.

6 Lay the lace on your work surface, right side down, and lay the satin on top, also right side down. Pin the excess lace onto the back of the satin and stitch in place, about 1cm (½in) in from the edges. If you should have some lace with a scalloped edge, incorporate it into the design. Here, only three sides are stitched together, leaving the scalloped edge loose.

Embroidering small motifs onto handkerchiefs, pillowcases or napkins is a really satisfying and relatively quick way to give new fabric a vintage feel. The detail on these embroidered napkins adds a perfect finishing touch to your table setting. The instructions here are for one napkin; repeat as many times as you need.

Embroidered & tasselled napkins

you will need

Plain cotton or linen cut into a 30cm (12in) square

Sewing machine (optional)

Embroidery design (see page 224)

Tracing paper: 15cm (6in) piece

Embroidery thread in a contrasting colour

Embroidery hoop (optional)

1 silk tassel in a colour that matches the embroidery thread

1 Press in 3mm (⅛in) and then 5mm (¼in) all the way around the square of fabric. Stitch in place with slip stitch (see page 208) or use a sewing machine.

2 Copy the pattern on page 224 or your own pattern onto the tracing paper and then pin it to the napkin about 2.5cm (1in) in from one corner. Work small running stitches with a contrasting colour of thread carefully through both layers around all the outlines, except for any tiny details, which you can stitch by hand when you have embroidered the rest of the design. Gently remove the tracing paper.

3 If you are using an embroidery hoop, place it around the design and gently pull the fabric taut.

4 Separate the embroidery thread into three strands and, using tiny back stitches, embroider the design onto the linen. To separate the threads, cut a length of embroidery thread from the skein roughly twice the length of your forearm and gently separate out the strands by running your thumb down the thread, making sure you continue to hold the two groups tightly.

5 When you have finished stitching, remove the hoop.

6 Pin a tassel to the corner beneath the embroidery and stitch in place using a cross-stitch. Iron the napkin on the wrong side to finish.

PEARLS of WISDOM

I have used a plain piece of linen but the embroidery would work equally well on a patterned background if stitched in a contrasting colour.

These raggedy rose napkin ties go perfectly with the embroidered napkins. The instructions here are for one tie; repeat as many times as you need. I recommend using fabric offcuts to create a set of perfect English roses for your table.

Raggedy rose napkin ties

you will need

23 x 5.5cm (9 x 2¼in) fabric for each tie, plus offcuts to cover the wire and finish the ends

36cm (14in) soft wire

Double-sided sticky tape

1 Along one long side of the fabric (the bottom, if there's a right way to the pattern), 5mm (¼in) in from the edge, sew a loose running stitch (see page 208). Don't finish off at the end, but remove the needle and gently pull up the thread to gather the fabric. Don't cut the thread.

2 Starting at the narrow end opposite the loose thread, fold it over by a few millimetres and then wrap the gathered fabric around itself to make a roll. Wind the thread around the outside of the tie at least six times to secure the material and to give the flower an attractive binding. By this time, it should look like a flower just opening. Stitch together firmly at the bottom to ensure that it won't unravel.

3 Cover the wire by cutting a narrow piece from an offcut of fabric that is long enough to wind around and cover the full length of the wire. Stick double-sided sticky tape along the full length of the fabric on the wrong side, then tightly wrap it around the wire.

4 Attach the fabric-covered wire to the underside of the flower with a few neat stitches, and also stitch the fabric closed at the ends of the wire.

5 As an attractive addition to the end of each wire, you could make small decorative miniature versions of the main flower. Cut two very narrow strips of the same fabric about 5cm (2in) long and 1cm (½in) wide and preferably in the same fabric as the flower head. Gently gather as in Step 1 and make as in Step 2. Push each one onto the ends of the wire and stitch to the fabric covering to secure.

PEARLS *of* WISDOM

A lavender tip placed between the tie and the cutlery or napkin will add a sense of occasion.

Vintage Garden

I love the look of the indoors out of doors. Unfortunately we don't get to spend many days or evenings outdoors in this country, as the weather is frequently against us, but whenever we can do it, I'm out there!

The romantic in me loves the idea of a scene in the garden that's rather like something from *A Midsummer Night's Dream* – a fantastical, magical world set amongst nature. When Danny and I were planning our wedding in 2006, I decided I wanted exactly that sort of look, and with the help of my friend Alex, who is a stylist on *Elle Decoration*, we dreamed up a scheme of armoires and chandeliers nestling amongst the trees and foliage, along with pianos stuffed with fresh flowers. As the plans escalated, so did my fears about English weather, and we ended up dropping the idea (the day dawned bright and hot, of course!). I have created a scaled-down version of this design since then, and it looked fantastic!

In the garden, less is definitely more. Don't overdo the look and instead let nature speak for itself as much as possible – even the simplest scheme can look magical outside. You don't need a mature, landscaped garden; even the most bland space can look brilliant with the right accessories. You can set up a tent outdoors and brighten up boring canvas with colourful throws or fringing. If you don't have a tent, you can create one by hanging bedspreads and rugs over ropes suspended from branches. For special occasions, there are even companies who hire out vintage marquees of all sizes.

For more impromptu entertaining in the garden, just bring out tables and chairs and decorate them with pretty tablecloths and jam jars of freshly picked flowers, or spread rugs or floral quilts over the ground and cover them with scatter cushions of all different shapes and sizes. I think French wrought-iron tables look wonderful outside, but you can just bring out wooden chairs from the kitchen if that's what you have. A little floral fabric bunting in the trees looks pretty during the day, and by night you can hang fairy lights or lanterns amongst the branches. If you don't have trees, hang lights wherever you can and place lanterns on the floor around your rugs, and scatter tea lights over the table. Add in a campfire or a fire pit and a few friends and you will find you have stepped back in time to a perfect vintage picnic!

Bunting is great for outdoor parties. I like to put a vintage twist on the traditional variety with lace, tassels and vintage linens and handkerchiefs, all of which you can easily track down online, in charity shops or at antique fairs. Each of these designs makes 3m (3yd) of bunting with an extra 50cm (20in) tie at each end.

Vintage linen bunting

Traditional bunting with a twist

you will need

1m (1yd) each of three or four mismatched vintage fabrics, enough for 20 triangles
Card triangle template: 18 x 25 x 25cm (7 x 10 x 10in)
Dressmaker's chalk
4m (13ft) bias tape
Sewing machine (optional)
3m (3yd) tasselled braid
1m (1yd) striped narrow ribbon

1 Lay out your fabrics, wrong side up, and place the template on top. Draw around the template with the dressmaker's chalk. Repeat for twice as many flags as you need. This method uses 10 flags, so 20 triangles are needed; increase or decrease the number of flags depending on the length of bunting you wish to make.

2 For each flag, pin together two triangles with right sides facing. Stitch along the two longer sides taking a 1cm (½in) seam allowance, then turn through and press, turning in the seam allowance on the short edge.

3 Leaving about 50cm (20in) of bias tape free at each end for tying up, fold the bias tape in half and pin the flags along the bias at about 15cm (6in) intervals and between the two layers of the bias tape. Check the spacing by eye and tweak if necessary before stitching the flags to the tape using running stich (see page 208), or use a sewing machine.

4 Pin and then stitch the tasselled braid to the bias tape over the front of the flags.

5 Cut the ribbon in half and stitch to each end of the bias tape to create a tie to hang the bunting.

PEARLS *of* WISDOM

Before you commit to sewing the pinned flags to the bias tape, hold up the bunting and check their spacing by eye.

Lace & doily bunting

you will need

About 12 mismatched vintage doilies

4m (13ft) vintage ivory braid

Sewing machine (optional)

1 Fold each doily in half and press with an iron, then place each one over the braid so it sits inside the fold. Because vintage doilies tend to be rather heavy, this helps keep them secure.

2 Spread the doilies evenly along the braid and pin into place. Leave about 50cm (20in) of the ivory braid free at each end for tying it up. Hold up the bunting and check the spacing by eye before you commit to sewing. Make any tweaks and then hand stitch the linens to the braid using running stitch (see page 208) or use a sewing machine.

3 To finish, stitch together the bottom of each doily for extra security.

Handkerchief bunting

you will need

About 8 mismatched square linen handkerchiefs

4m (4yd) black lace edging

Sewing machine (optional)

4 large black tassels

1 Fold the handkerchiefs corner to corner to create a triangle and press with an iron.

2 Leaving about 50cm (20in) of lace free at each end for tying up, pin the handkerchiefs along the lace, equally spaced, and check the spacing by eye. Then sew the handkerchiefs to the lace with running stitch (see page 208) or using a sewing machine.

3 Stitch together the bottom of each handkerchief for extra security. Then pin and sew the tassels to the bottom point of alternate flags.

Nº2

Dream Living Space

Lace panels feature heavily in my house; they can be found hung at windows, on tables as covers, on chairs as throws and on beds as canopies. I absolutely adore the romantic feel they give. Hanging a single lace panel at the window will diffuse light and provide a little privacy as well as giving a soft and delicate look to the room.

Lace window panel

you will need

Lace panel, to match the size of your window

Sewing machine (optional)

Net curtain wire with eye hooks at each end to fit the width of your window frame

2 screw eyes

1 Choose a panel that is the same width as the window so that the attractive edging needn't be cut off. Cut the panel so that it is about 7.5cm (3in) longer than the height of the window.

2 For the top hem, press in 1cm (½in) and then 4cm (1¾in) and stitch with a running stitch (see page 208) or use a sewing machine close to the inside folded edge. Pin in place and stitch along the double folded fabric. Don't stitch up the sides of the hem, so that you can slide the curtain wire through. Stitch a very narrow double hem at the bottom of the panel. If it has scalloped edges, the panel won't need hemming at the sides.

3 Thread the panel onto the net curtain wire and hang at the window frame using the screw eyes.

PEARLS *of* WISDOM

If you would like your panel a specific colour, you can easily dye white lace by hand.
For practical romance, make the lace a blackout panel by fitting a plain white or neutral roller blind behind it.

Luscious Lace

Anyone who knows my designs can't fail to realise that I love lace. Just one piece of strategically placed lace can turn the day-to-day into something decadent, and make the ordinary seem glamorous – at very little cost. And who doesn't want a little inexpensive glamour in their life?

My love affair with lace began when I first discovered Stevie Nicks, who made wearing lace and chiffon rock-star cool during the 1970s and 1980s. Growing up I was a classic Goth – my signature style was black boots and black lace, topped off with a red velvet hat. Ever since, lace has been a vital ingredient for me – whether in the home or on clothes – and I can't get enough of it.

So it isn't surprising that it was that single lace curtain that set my change in career from singing to vintage design in motion, and I still make dyed curtains to order now, just as I did back then. Although I first started using lace in the home as curtains, I was never going to confine it to one purpose. That's the beauty of this fabric; you can use it anywhere you like: as tablecloths or runners, on furniture, on coffee tables, or draped over curtain poles or bedheads – wherever you think it looks good. It doesn't have to be obvious, either, just a fragment here and there adds femininity and grace to a room – try hanging vintage lace dresses on pretty fabric-covered hangers from the doors of wardrobes or on walls.

Lace adds drama and elegance to the boudoir when draped over bedspreads or quilts, and I have used it several times to cover the top and sides of a four-poster bed. Used this way, you do need one long piece of lace, otherwise it can look odd if there are panels sewn together. Also, if you want to use lace on sofas, make sure it is fairly thick to prevent tears, and add fringing or tassels around the edge to stop it

getting 'lost'. Equally, for curtains, make sure the piece you buy is big enough to cover the window, and choose one that has no damage to it, as any holes or pulls will be more obvious when the panel is dyed and hung up against the light.

Smaller pieces of lace are ideal for covering lampshades (see page 84), for upcycling cushion covers (see page 63) or for decorating silk or satin covers with lace butterflies, hearts or whatever shape takes your fancy (see page 113). You can also make lavender hearts from fabric and lace to hang on walls, armoires and wardrobes, which look pretty and have a practical, fragrant purpose (see page 133).

Although I love lace, I don't like it when it's white, so I dye virtually every piece I get hold of. When I first started doing this I had a washing machine in my house that I kept specifically for the purpose, but that's not necessary if you only want to do the odd piece. If the lace is cotton, this can be dyed using any of the wonderful range of Dylon colours.

Simply put the lace in the drum of any washing machine with the dye and set to a 40-degree cycle. (Be careful to make sure nothing is in the drum when you start dyeing, or else you'll end up with one dyed sock or similar!) Once the fabric is dyed, make sure you run a 90-degree cycle with just a washing tab in the machine to clean the drum before you chuck in your laundry.

Be bold with colour when you are dyeing lace – pastels look great for shabby-chic style, black really works for a bit of gothic glamour, while dark reds or burgundies look rich and more masculine.

If you need a large piece of lace, you might find it easier to buy modern lace because you will be more likely to get a piece cut to the right size – department stores or haberdashery shops will stock lace in rolls. But if size isn't such an issue, you will have more choice of patterns if you get hold of gorgeous vintage designs. Decent-sized scraps are surprisingly cheap to buy – if you're willing to rummage through fabric offcuts, you can often find charity shops, auction houses and flea markets selling pieces for small amounts of money. Look online, too. As with anything vintage, if you see a beautiful piece of lace, buy it – you may never see the like again and you will be able to find a use for it somewhere – trust me!

Changing your soft furnishings is the easiest way to instantly refresh a room. One of the simplest and most affordable ways you can do this is with cushions; upcycle with trims or other embellishments, or make your own creations to showcase your favourite fabrics or embroidery. Don't be afraid to mix patterns, but consider the colour tones.

Cushion covers galore

Heart-shaped cushion

you will need

2 pieces of 45 x 45cm (18 x 18in) satin fabric
2 pieces of 45 x 45cm (18 x 18in) lace
40cm- (16in)-wide heart-shaped cushion pad
Dressmaker's chalk
114 x 7cm (45 x 2¾in) lace edging
Sewing machine (optional)
50 x 2.5cm (20 x 1in) black satin ribbon
50cm x 3mm (20 x ⅛in) black satin ribbon
4 beads, for threading onto the narrow satin ribbon

1 Lay out both pieces of satin fabric and cover with both pieces of lace (it doesn't matter if the fabric is right side up or down). Pin the layers together all over. Then lay the cushion pad over the top in the centre of the fabric and draw around the edge with dressmaker's chalk, adding a 1cm (½in) seam allowance. Cut out the heart shapes and separate the layers.

2 To stitch the layers and the lace edging together, lay them out in the following order:

Satin heart (right side up)
Lace heart
Lace edging with the shaped outside edge facing towards the centre of the heart; tack these layers together around the outer edge
Lace heart
Satin heart (right side down)

Ensure all edges are aligned, and pin together.

3 Sew the layers together with a small running stitch (or use a sewing machine), leaving a 1cm (½in) seam allowance (taking care to ensure the lace edging isn't caught in the stitching). Start at the bottom of the heart and stitch all around, stopping about 20cm (8in) before you reach the end. Trim the seam and turn right side out.

4 Insert the cushion pad and then close the opening with slip stitch (see page 208).

5 Decorate the cushion with the satin ribbons. Tie the wider ribbon into a bow and stitch it in the middle to prevent the bow from coming undone, then stitch the bow onto the centre of the heart's 'V'. Fold the narrow ribbon in half and then in half again. Stitch together in the centre to hold and then stitch onto the bottom of the cushion. Snip through the loop to leave four separate pieces of ribbon. Thread the beads onto one loose end and tie a knot to prevent them falling off.

Lace bolster cushion

you will need

36 x 15cm (15 x 6in) bolster cushion pad
60 x 36cm (24 x 15in) satin fabric
Sewing machine (optional)
60 x 54cm (24 x 21in) lace, plus small offcuts for the buttons
2 x 3cm (1¼in) diameter self-covering buttons

Continues...

1 To line the bolster cushion, fold the satin fabric in half along its width with right sides facing, so that you have a rectangle that measures 30 x 36cm (12 x 15in).

2 Stitch together the longer edge using running stitch (see page 208), or use a sewing machine. Trim the seam and turn right side out. Pull the sleeve onto the bolster cushion pad so that only the ends of the bolster remain uncovered.

3 For the lace cover, press in a 5mm (¼in) hem to the wrong side on each shorter edge and then fold once more by 1.5cm (⅝in). Press again, then pin and stitch. Fold the lace fabric in half along its width with right sides facing. This time you will have a rectangle that measures 30 x 51cm (12 x 20¼in). Stitch the cover and pull onto the bolster as in Step 2, ensuring the excess fabric is an equal length at each end.

4 Cover the buttons with the lace offcuts following the manufacturer's instructions.

5 To gather the fabric at the ends, thread a double length of thread onto a needle and make loose running stitches along the seam at one end of the lace cover. It is important to ensure that the thread is secured tightly. When you get back to the beginning of the seam, gently pull the thread to gather the seam as much as you can. You will be able to push this down onto the centre of the bolster end. Stitch the gathered end together very firmly to prevent it from coming undone, then cover the end by sewing on one of the self-covered buttons. Repeat this step for the other end of the bolster.

Vintage linen cushions

you will need

2 pieces of fabric, 53cm (21½in) square
53cm (21½in) lace trim, about 12.5cm (5in) wide
Sewing machine (optional)
50cm (20in) zip, in a contrasting colour if you want to make a feature of it
50cm (20in) square cushion pad

1 Cut one of the fabric squares in half. Along one cut edge, with the right side up, pin and then tack the lace trim to the fabric. Along each of the edges you have just cut (including the lace-trimmed edge), press in 5mm (¼in) and then 1cm (½in) and stitch close to the inside folded edge with running stitch (see page 208), or use a sewing machine. These will form the centre back (or front if you want to make a feature of the lace decoration and contrasting coloured zip) of the cushion, joined by the zip. Lay them face down on your work surface, with the hems about 1cm (½in) apart.

2 Lay the zip over the gap between the fabric pieces, right side down, and pin and tack the zip to both sides of the cushion back, maintaining the 1cm (½in) gap so that the zip will be clearly seen when the cushion cover is finished. Stitch the zip to the fabric using back stitch (see page 209) or a sewing machine. Remove the tacking thread.

3 Pin the front and back pieces together, with right sides facing. Use either end of the zip as a guide to where to start pinning. The seam of the cushion should be in line with each end of the zip, which is about 2cm (¾in) in from the edge of your fabric.

4 Stitch the cushion pieces together, taking a 1.5cm (⅝in) seam allowance. Cut off any excess fabric from the sides and corners, turn right side out and stuff with the cushion pad.

Retro-print appliqué cushion

Bondaweb (fusible webbing): enough for the size of your cut-out motif(s)
Patterned fabric with obvious images
Cushion cover: a 58cm (23in) square cushion cover was used here

1 Lay the Bondaweb over the fabric and cut out sufficient webbing to cover the image you are going to appliqué to the cushion cover. Make sure the piece of Bondaweb that you are left with is slightly smaller than the overall size of the fabric or else it will stick to your ironing board cover and make a sticky mess.

2 Lay the fabric on your ironing board, right side down, and place the trimmed Bondaweb over the part of the fabric that you will be appliquéing, with the adhesive side (the 'rough' side) facing the fabric. With a medium-hot iron, press the Bondaweb onto the fabric.

3 Once cool, cut the fabric motif neatly to shape. Peel off the paper layer of the Bondaweb, then position the fabric on the cushion cover, Bondaweb side down. Lay a damp cloth over the top. Press the appliqué onto the cushion until the fabric of the cushion has bonded with the appliqué. This should only take a few seconds, but it's always good to check the manufacturer's instructions, too.

4 To finish, you can either leave the appliqué un-stitched or add a blanket stitch for decoration (see page 208). Repeat with more appliqué if you wish.

Cushions & Quilts

Often it is the details that make a room, and accessories such as quilts and cushions can really enhance a vintage look while at the same time echoing the mood you want to create. It seems such a simple thing, but it's something that you can get so wrong if you don't give it a bit of thought.

Quilts are beautiful objects that add instant interest to a room, and the old ones in particular just ooze history and romance because of the wonderful fabrics used in them – the prints of some have even inspired some of my dress designs. You can make your own quilt – a great use for vintage fabric offcuts – but vintage quilts can also be found in all the usual places and may be cheaper than some modern handmade versions. If you prefer new ones, they can be found in department stores or online. Some old quilts can be a little marked or smelly (usually just a mothy, dusty smell rather than anything unpleasant), but most can be washed in a washing machine on a gentle hand-wash setting, or you can have them dry cleaned by specialists. Check with whoever is selling the quilt before you have it cleaned; they should be able to advise you.

Quilts have traditionally been used as bedspreads, but why stop there? They look beautiful draped over the ends of beds or over chairs or linen chests, and some people lay them on sofas, but this works better if the quilt is not too bulky. Quilts also work well on the wall, hung up as they are or in frames, or thrown over a banister rail. If you

buy a slightly damaged vintage quilt, display it with its best face out –
they look really pretty folded and piled up in glass-fronted cupboards,
especially if there are a few together in different patterns and colours.
The only advice I would give is don't buy quilts if you have cats – my
feline friends love curling up in them, but they also love scratching them.

Just as quilts can add colour and texture to a monochrome room,
so too can cushions, and often the two work well together. There is a
temptation to go mad with cushions and scatter them everywhere – on
sofas, chairs, the floor, window seats, you name it – but try to rein in that
urge. Few things suggest luxury and comfort like cushions and quilts,
but you need to keep the overall effect uncluttered if you want an
inviting, relaxing feel. Cushions look best when grouped together, but
don't use too many in one place – on chairs or sofas, in particular, they
all end up falling on the floor or leaving you with no space to sit down.
Alternatively, if you prefer a simpler look, just use one or two as a focal
point and to pep up a plain sofa.

When grouping cushions, keep them all roughly the same size for
a less messy look and just mix and match their shapes and colours.
However, don't overdo it with too many patterns or colours. In white
rooms, cushions can denote the colour scheme, but where there is
wallpaper or paint on the walls, the cushions should reflect this and not
clash. Ideally, use cushions that share a common colour in their patterns
so they have some unity, particularly when the room has a specific
colour scheme. Try to blend fabrics and textures, too; for instance, silk
looks glamorous with lace, but odd with tapestry, while tapestry looks
great with velvet. Cushion covers are an obvious area where you can
upcycle – with a little lace, ribbon or fringing you can add interest to a
less-exciting cushion, or make it work with the look of your room.

Cushions, and particularly bolster cushions, add romance and movie-
style glamour to a bedroom, particularly when they are made from silk
or lace, or they can make a bed look pretty and inviting if they have a
feminine pattern. You need to be a little practical here too, and not go
mad in a quest to create a luxurious look; keep cushions on a bed to a
minimum, as heaving loads on and off the bed every time you use it can
be a bit of a pain.

Wherever you use them, choose cushions and quilts that you
especially like and use them as an opportunity to add a really personal
touch to your design. Go glam, go cosy, go seductive … or just go with
what you love to add the final flourish to your style.

Being able to relax and put your feet up after a long day is one of life's little luxuries; this footstool will help you do just that. Here a gypsy rose inspired design is cross-stitched onto vintage linen – copy this design or create one of your own.

Upcycled gypsy rose footstool

you will need

Old footstool

Sandpaper and paint of your choice (optional) (see page 210)

4oz density polyester quilting wadding (optional)

Spray glue (optional)

Hot glue gun

Vintage linen: measuring about 1m (1yd) square

30 x 17cm (12 x 6½in) piece of 14-count soluble canvas

15cm (6in) embroidery hoop (optional)

Cross-stitch pattern (see page 225)

Cotton embroidery threads

Towel

Staple gun

Fabric: enough to back the underside of the footstool

Heavyweight fusible interfacing

1 On a prepared work surface, turn the footstool upside down and remove the feet. Then remove the old fabric and backing together with any nails and staples from the woodwork. If your footstool is old and battered, you might want to give it a lick of paint (see page 210). If necessary, cut out some new wadding to fit the top and stick it in place with spray glue or using the hot glue gun.

2 Lay the linen on a flat surface and mark with pins where you want the pattern to appear. Then pin and tack the soluble canvas onto the linen in the same place. If you are using an embroidery hoop, place it around the soluble canvas and gently pull the fabric taut.

3 Stitch the pattern using cross stitches following the chart (see page 225). You will only need to stitch with two strands of the thread. To separate them, cut a length of embroidery thread from the skein roughly twice the length of your forearm and gently separate out the strands by running your thumb down the thread, making sure you continue to hold the two groups tightly.

4 When you have finished stitching, remove the hoop and the tacking stitches.

Continues...

Upcycled gypsy rose footstool

5 Soak the embroidered material in a bowl of clean lukewarm water for around 10 minutes until all the soluble canvas has dissolved and you are left with just your stitches. Leave the linen to dry naturally, laying it flat on a towel.

6 Once dry (or nearly dry), turn your embroidery face down on a towel and iron on the back to ensure that you don't crush your stitches with the iron.

7 Lay the linen over the top of the footstool, ensuring the pattern is positioned correctly. Holding the fabric firmly in place, flip the footstool top over and use the staple gun to fix the fabric in place. Work on one edge at a time, always starting in the centre and working out to the edges, and keeping the fabric taut.

8 Cut off any excess fabric at the corners and place staples along the remaining edges, remembering to keep the tension even. Trim any excess material.

9 Cut the backing fabric to the same size as the back of the stool, add 2cm (1in) to each dimension. Finish the backing by covering it with the fusible interfacing following the manufacturer's instructions. Press in 1cm (½in) on each edge and glue to the underside of the stool, hiding the staples and raw edges of the embroidered fabric.

10 Screw the feet back on, turn the footstool over and put your feet up!

PEARLS *of* WISDOM

You could also add a sequin, braid or pompom trim around the edge of the footstool cushion for extra detail.

ADD
A BIT
of
elegance
TO AN
EVERYDAY
item

50s
wallpapered
coffee table

With its wonderful range of patterns, colours and styles – vintage or new – I never throw away offcuts of wallpaper; they always come in handy. It's easy to attach wallpaper to just about any surface with craft glue or wallpaper paste, and it's a simple and stylish way to transform your furniture. Whoever said wallpaper was just for walls?

you will need

Occasional or side table

Your choice of wallpaper: enough to cover your chosen surface

Pencil

Scissors or craft knife

Wallpaper paste and brush

1 Place the wallpaper face up, on the top of the table (or whatever object you are covering) and mark lightly with a pencil where you need to cut it out. If the wallpaper has a bold design, check that it is positioned in an appropriate place – centred or aligned with one of the edges, for example. It also needs to be straight.

2 Cut around the lines with scissors or a craft knife. Protect your work surface and make up the wallpaper paste, then brush it onto the back of the paper.

3 Stick the paper onto the table; you can move the paper around gently, but be careful, as paste temporarily weakens the paper.

4 Brush paste over the top of the paper to seal it. Apply a layer and allow it to dry, then repeat two or three times to build up a protective coat. Leave the table to dry for at least 5 hours.

Trinket tray

This is a really quick way to upcycle a picture frame, whether it's one you've had lying around for ages or one you've bought specially. Use the tray to hold vases or perfume bottles, or sit your keys or telephone on. This is one of my favourite projects because it is pretty and ornate, yet so simple to make.

you will need

Ornate vintage or vintage-style wooden picture frame, roughly 40 x 60cm (16 x 24in)
Your choice of fabric, the same size as the glass in your frame
Pins or dressmaker's chalk
Hot glue gun
2 small drawer handles
Tacks
Hammer
45mm- (1¾in)-wide masking/sealing tape (optional)

1 Remove the glass from the picture frame and dispose of it safely. Remove the stiff board from the back of the picture frame together with any tacks or tape if it is an old frame.

2 Lay the fabric over the board, centring the design if necessary. Mark the edge of the board on the fabric with pins or dressmaker's chalk and then cut the fabric to size.

3 Using the hot glue gun, stick the fabric to the inside of the backing board.

4 Attach the handles to the front of the frame, one on each side as in the photograph. Use tacks and hammer them in place. Put the board back into the frame and secure with the existing tacks. For greater durability, replace the glass. Secure the board more firmly by stapling it into the frame or by using the masking/sealing tape.

PEARLS *of* WISDOM

You could swap the fabric for wallpaper, varnished with craft glue or wallpaper paste to give durability.

Smouldering Lighting

A ny interior designer of any style will tell you that lighting is the
most important element in any room scheme – the right lighting
can make even a blank canvas seem exciting and interesting.
Before you decide on the type of lighting you want, think about the
mood you want to create in the room, and what its natural light level is
like. For example, our sitting room is quite dark, even in summer, but
I like it to have a cosy feel, so we have a few standard lamps around for
subtle, subdued lighting and to reflect the mood. Of course, if you want
much more light in a darker room, you could add overhead lighting
and a few carefully placed lamps on tables and bookcases. Bright,
lightly decorated rooms filled with natural light may need less lighting,
or perhaps just an overhead shade. Rooms with low ceilings are better
illuminated with low-level lights or lamps, whereas rooms with high
ceilings just cry out for fabulous chandeliers.

Sometimes you will find a lamp that shouts 'buy me', but you just
can't think where it will go. Follow your instincts – you might find that
that lamp then dictates the whole look of a room. It happened to me
when I fell in love with a 1920s standard lamp I saw in Paris; it had a
beautiful, black wrought-iron base topped with a pale cream shade
fringed with hanging tassels, which had gorgeous beading on them.
As with all things vintage, anything I buy has to have character and
history, both of which this lamp had in spades. I couldn't get on the
train without it, so much to his annoyance Danny had to help me get
it back to England, where it became my muse for the sitting room.

If you do go for lamps, keep them simple: mix and match with a few

beautiful and unique lampstands and shades, but don't use too many different styles in one room or you will create a messy look. I have a beautiful blue peacock-fringe lamp in my dressing room by designer Zoë Darlington. When choosing lamps, remember that the stand is as important as the shade. Sometimes you might find just a stand or a shade you love in a vintage flea market or shop, so if you come across such a thing, buy it – you can find the other bit later. If you have a stand and no shade, you could even buy a modern shade that fits it and upcycle it with lace or fringing to get the vintage look you want (see page 84).

When buying vintage lights, or even some modern lights, there are a few dos and don'ts you should first bear in mind. Do try to see the light before you buy it, and preferably get someone to demonstrate it. There's nothing worse than getting a light home only to find it doesn't work. Be wary, too, of lights that need specialist fitting, and get a quote before you commit to the light – you could find that the cost of having it fitted ends up being a lot more than you spend on the light. If you are buying a chandelier, make sure it is not too heavy for your ceiling, and that you have access to a joist from which you can hang it. For any vintage light fitting, also make sure that you can easily get bulbs that will work in it, so you can replace them when they blow.

Your lighting scheme should reflect your personality as much as any other feature of your design, so go with what really takes your fancy – rules are made to be broken! Aside from formal lighting, I often find that a string of fairy lights or candles can be the perfect finishing touch.

I love chandeliers, from small, simple candelabras to large crystal centrepieces, and have sourced and restored many vintage chandeliers over the years. If you haven't got a large enough room or the budget to buy a genuine antique you can still get the look with these really simple ideas. And better still, your chandelier will be truly unique.

Beaded & jewelled dressed chandelier

you will need

Vintage-inspired candelabra-style chandelier

Cleaning cloth

Vintage accessories, including beads, brooches and necklaces, feathers, silk flowers, baubles; even little figurines – the more the merrier, but be careful to check the materials or components to ensure that they are fireproof

Plastic-coated garden wire

Wire cutters

1 Give your chandelier a good clean, then hang it in the place where it will live (for the time being, at least – I am always moving mine around). This will help you to get a sense of proportion. You don't want to add too many adornments and make the chandelier appear too 'heavy' for the space it's hanging in. To decorate, bring the chandelier down to your work surface.

2 Start with accessories that will hang and drape from the chandelier, such as the beads and necklaces. Hang them carefully, layering as you go, but not in a uniform way. Then add your smaller accessories – the brooches, ornaments, feathers and other finishing touches.

3 Don't be afraid to experiment – you can always swap things around. When you are happy with the end result, use short lengths of garden wire to fix everything discreetly into place. Ensure that neither the objects nor the wire are too close to any light bulbs or candles.

I am something of a magpie when it comes to lampshades – whether they are adorned with droplets and tassels or heavily patterned and ornately shaped. This fringed two-tone shade is a great way to capture vintage style in your home. I would recommend using a plain circular lampshade rather than a more ornate one, to make this project less fiddly.

Two-tone lampshade

you will need

Lampshade frame

Heavily patterned fabric: enough to fit twice around the inside of the shade

Plain cotton or linen fabric: enough to fit around the outside of the shade

Black lace or voile: enough to fit around the outside of the shade

Sewing machine (optional)

Hot glue gun

Long black tassel fringe: enough to fit twice around the circumference of the shade

1 Source a lampshade from a secondhand or charity shop or upcycle one of your own. You only need the frame, so if there is fabric already on the lampshade, remove it.

2 Measure the circumference and height of the lampshade and cut out both sets of fabric and lace as follows:

    Heavily patterned fabric: double the
      circumference x the height + 2.5cm (1in)
    Plain cotton or linen: the circumference
      + 2.5cm (1in) x the height + 2.5cm (1in)
    Lace: the circumference x the height
      + 2.5cm (1in)

3 Along both long edges of the heavily patterned inner fabric, fold and pin pleats at 1cm (½in) intervals until you have a pleated strip that measures slightly longer than the circumference of the lampshade. Stitch along the bottom and top edges with running stitch (see page 208) or using a sewing machine to keep the pleats in place.

4 Heat the glue gun and apply the glue to the top and bottom of one section of the inside of the frame. Making sure the pleats are facing inwards, swiftly stick the top and bottom hems onto the frame, wrapping the material slightly over the top and bottom. You may find another pair of hands useful here as the hot glue gun is only effective if the material is applied when the glue is very hot. Repeat by gluing the next section of the frame until you have entirely covered it. Overlap the excess length to finish it off.

5 Attach the plain outer fabric to the outside of the lampshade. Apply the glue to the top and bottom of the frame, sticking the plain outer fabric over the patterned fabric, sandwiching the frame in between. Keep the plain fabric taut as you stick it in place around the outside of the shade and finish by overlapping one edge over the other.

6 Place the lace over the plain fabric, neatly wrapping the excess over the top and bottom of the frame and glue in place as in Step 5.

7 Attach the fringe to the bottom of the lampshade by first applying the glue in small sections and then pulling the fringe around onto it. For a luxurious feel, the fringe on this lampshade has been wrapped around twice.

Pressed flowers calendar

You may have guessed already that I am a very big fan of flowers, from delicate displays in jam jars to big bold hydrangeas, peonies and roses, but also floral wallpaper, floral printed fabric and lace with floral patterns. Pressed and dried flowers are also beautiful to display, as in this calendar, or simply framed or used on homemade cards. It's also very easy to make your own press.

2 pieces of plywood, each measuring 34 x 25cm (13½ x 10in)
Cordless drill
16 1.5cm (⅝in) diameter washers
8 5.2cm (2¼in) screws
4 A4 sheets of corrugated cardboard
6 A4 sheets of blotting paper
8 butterfly wing nuts
Vintage fabric or wallpaper, to decorate the plywood
Braid, to decorate the plywood
Hot glue gun
Flowers and leaves for pressing

1 On a prepared work surface and following the manufacturer's instructions, mark and then drill four equally spaced holes down each side of both pieces of plywood. Keep them close to the edge so that the screws won't touch the cardboard and card inside the flower press.

2 Take the bottom piece of plywood and thread a washer onto a screw. Push it up through one of the holes. Repeat for each of the remaining seven holes. Layer the cardboard and paper, starting with a layer of cardboard topped with two pieces of blotting paper. Continue to add layers of cardboard and paper, finishing with a sheet of cardboard. Top with the remaining piece of plywood, threading the screws through the holes. Add another washer to each screw and finish with a butterfly wing nut.

3 Decorate the press covers with the fabric or wallpaper and stick braid around the edge using a hot glue gun. Once the glue is dry you can press your leaves and flowers.

4 Suggestions for flowers that are good to press include apple and cherry blossom, gypsophila, clover, cranesbill, heather, larkspur and pansies. For greenery, consider maple, virginia creeper and weeping willow leaves, as these all have varied and beautiful shapes. Ivy, fern and artemisia leaves also press very well.

5 Make sure your specimens are trimmed and 100 per cent clean and dry. Undo the butterfly wing nuts and remove the top of your press, followed by the top three layers of cardboard and paper. Lay as many leaves and flowers as you can without them overlapping on the bottom piece of blotting paper. Cover with the second piece of blotting paper, as before, and then continue to build up the layers, but this time positioning the leaves and flowers between the layers of blotting paper.

6 Thread the screws through the holes of the top piece of plywood, then add the washers and butterfly wing nuts and tighten as much as you are able. Label the press with the date, as it is so easy to forget when you put the flowers in. Leave them to dry for about 4 weeks.

7 Use the template on page 226 to create a calendar so you can admire your pressed flowers all year round.

PEARLS *of* WISDOM

Pick perfect blooms in their prime on a dry day. Never press flowers that are past their best; put half-dead flowers into a press and you'll get half-dead flowers afterwards.

Here are a couple of my favourite floral decorations – a full-bloom summer wreath and a dried flower heart-shaped wreath, which makes the perfect Christmas decoration. They are both very different, but the method is the same, and lots of fun. All of the materials you need will be available from your local florist.

Floral wreaths

Midsummer's dream wreath

you will need

Oasis foam wreath ring
Florist wire
Lace, ribbon or twine offcuts
Flowers and greenery, such as gypsophila, roses, hydrangea, scabiosa (flowers and seedheads), lavender, flowering mint and rosemary

1 Fully submerge the oasis in a bucket or sink full of water. Leave it for a couple of minutes until soaked through.

2 Wrap a length of the wire around the wreath ring and then twist it into a hook. Conceal the wire with some lace, ribbon or twine.

3 Start decorating the wreath by inserting greenery all around it. Push the stems (trimmed if necessary) into the oasis to the required depth and check that they are evenly spread around the wreath. The wreath shown here has about three times as many flowers in it as it does greenery.

4 Select the largest flowers, trim their stems to an appropriate length and insert them into the oasis. Depending on the weight of the flower head, you could also fix the largest flowers into the oasis with wire for support. Take a length of florist wire and wrap it around the stem, leaving the wire ends free to anchor into the oasis.

5 Insert smaller flowers, and then finally fill any gaps with soft small flower heads, such as the gypsophila and lavender. They support the other flowers and create a sense of balance.

6 Now you are ready to hang your wreath. Hang it out of direct daylight and spray the flowers with water daily to keep them fresh. Also add a small amount of cold water every few days to the oasis to help keep it damp. Dribble it in slowly from a small watering can or jug. The oasis should be damp but not so wet that it starts dripping. The wreath will be quite heavy when it is finished, so ensure it is hung on a secure hook on a wall.

Winter heart wreath

you will need

Heart-shaped twig wreath
Florist wire
Lace, ribbon or twine offcuts
Dried flowers and greenery such as hydrangeas, berries, grasses, firs and holly

1 Follow the steps for the Midsummer's dream wreath, using pieces of florist wire to fix the dried flowers into the wreath.

2 Hang out of direct sunlight and keep indoors.

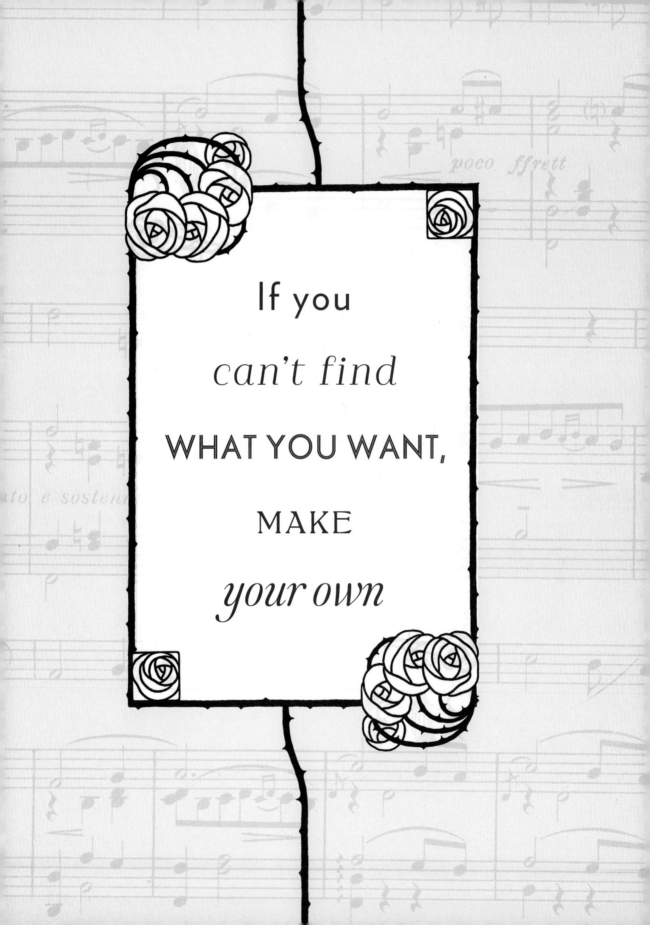

If you
can't find
WHAT YOU WANT,
MAKE
your own

Vintage Christmas

Capture the feel of a vintage Christmas with lace and velvet stockings hung by the fireplace; vintage-inspired handmade paper chains; lacy crackers at the Christmas table; and inspirational vintage decorations threaded onto decorative ribbons and hung from lights, trees, picture frames or door handles.

Lace Stockings

you will need

Stocking outline (see page 227)

Satin fabric: about 60cm (24in) square

Sewing machine (optional)

Lace or voile: about 60cm (24in) square

Decorative trimmings such as ribbons, fringes, buttons, sequins, beads, appliquéd motifs (optional)

1 Enlarge the stocking template on page 227 to the desired size on a photocopier and cut it out.

2 To make a lining for the stocking, cut out two stocking shapes from the satin fabric using the template. Sew the two stocking shapes together (use a sewing machine if you like) with right sides facing and with a 1cm (½in) seam allowance. Leave the top open. Trim the seams and turn right side out.

3 Cut out two more stocking shapes from the lace outer casing. Sew them together with a 1cm (½in) seam allowance and, again, leave the top open. Trim the seams and then turn right side out so the seams are on the inside.

4 Insert the satin stocking inside the lace stocking, aligning the seams. Turn in 1cm (½in) of the satin and lace at the top of the stocking so the hems are facing each other and you have neat edges. Stitch together with a sewing machine or by hand using slip stitch (see page 208). If you wish, you can then turn over about 4cm (1¾in) at the top to make a small cuff.

5 Sew on any decorative ribbons, fringes, buttons, sequins, beads or appliquéd motifs that you like. You could also use gold or silver thread to embroider a name onto the stocking, or simply leave it plain.

6 To hang the stocking, stitch a length of ribbon or lace onto the top of the back seam.

Paper chains

you will need

Strips of paper: leftover vintage-style wrapping paper or wallpaper offcuts, each about 2cm (¾in) wide and 7.5cm (3in) long; the chain in the picture uses 30 strips

Glue, double-sided sticky tape or a stapler

1 Take one of the strips of paper and paste, tape or staple the ends together to form a loop.

2 String a second strip of paper through the newly-made loop. Again, join the ends of the strip together with glue, tape or staples.

3 Continue until you reach the desired chain length. Hang the chain across ceilings and walls, or simply drape over mirrors and windows.

Vintage bauble place settings

you will need

Vintage baubles with wire loops: 1 per place setting
Cleaning cloth
Sticky-back foam pads
Card to make nameplates
Pen (or printer)
Sticky tape

1 Once you have sourced your baubles, give them a good clean, as the chances are that they have been tucked away in a cupboard for the last few years.

2 As baubles are round, attach a sticky-back foam pad to the bottom of each one so that it won't topple over.

3 Cut out 5 x 2cm (2 x ¾in) nameplates from the card. You don't want to make the top too weighty, so the smaller the card, the better. Then write the names of your guests in your neatest handwriting. If you don't trust your handwriting, print the names instead.

4 Attach a nameplate to the wire loop at the top of each bauble with some sticky tape and then set the baubles all around your Christmas dining table.

PEARLS *of* WISDOM

Make sure you pack your baubles away safely for the next year as they can easily break.

Lace Christmas crackers

you will need

Cracker template (see page 227)
Sufficient lightweight card for however many crackers you wish to make
Craft knife
Cutting mat
Cracker snaps
Double-sided sticky tape
String
Cracker gifts
Tissue paper
Colourful lace cut to the size of the cracker template
Coloured card or paper the size of the cracker template
Narrow ribbon, to finish

1 Enlarge the cracker template on page 227 on a photocopier to the desired size, and cut it out. Draw around the template onto the lightweight card however many times you need. Cut these shapes out too.

2 For each cracker, score along the dotted lines with a craft knife on a cutting mat and, also using a craft knife, cut out the diamond shapes. Fold the vertical and horizontal lines as shown on the template.

3 Tape a cracker snap at each end of the inside of the prepared card using double-sided sticky tape. Then roll the card into a cracker shape and join the edges with double-sided sticky tape. Tie one end with a length of string.

4 Wrap your gifts in some tissue paper and pop one inside each cracker. Then tie the other end with more string.

5 Wrap each cracker in decorative lace, placing coloured card or paper underneath in either a complementary or contrasting colour to set it off. Tie a piece of ribbon around each end of the cracker and finish in a bow.

Mini bunting

you will need

White lace or fabric offcuts, enough for 20 triangle flags
Card triangle template: 5 x 7.5 x 7.5cm (2 x 3 x 3in)
Dressmaker's chalk
2.5m (2½yd) white ribbon
Sewing machine (optional)

1 Lay out your lace or fabric offcuts, wrong side up, and place the template on top. Draw around the template with dressmaker's chalk for as many triangles as you need. For 1.5m (1½yd) of bunting, you need 20 flags. Cut around each one.

2 Pin each flag to the ribbon at close intervals and leaving 50cm (20in) of ribbon free at each end for hanging the bunting.

3 Stitch the flags onto the ribbon with a sewing machine or by hand using running stitch (see page 208). Ensure that the triangles sit behind the ribbon. Perfect mini bunting, ready to hang!

Lace-covered wooden heart & star baubles

you will need

8 pre-cut wooden hearts and stars
Cordless drill
Lace or fabric offcuts
Hot glue gun
4m (4yd) ribbon, the same thickness as the edge of the shapes to stick around them and for hanging

1 To make a hole in the top of each wooden shape for hanging, on a prepared work surface and following the manufacturer's instructions mark and then drill a small hole in each.

2 Lay out the lace or fabric on your work surface, wrong side up, and place each wooden shape on top. Draw around the shapes and cut out the fabric. You will need two pieces of fabric for each shape. Stick the cut-out fabric shapes to either side of the wooden shapes with the hot glue gun.

3 Measure the outer edge of a star and a heart and cut the lengths of ribbon required. Starting at the top of your shape stick the ribbon to the outer edge, again using the hot glue gun.

4 To hang the decorations, cut the remaining ribbon into eight equal lengths. Make a snip in the lace above the hole on each side, feed through a length of ribbon and tie.

PEARLS *of* WISDOM

Depending on your Christmas theme you could add extra embellishments, such as sequins and glitter.

№ 3

Bedroom
Delights

✝

The right headboard can transform a bed, or even a whole bedroom. This luxurious padded headboard was such a success I decided to cover an ottoman in a similar way (see page 106). You might choose to match the fabric of the headboard and the ottoman if they are in the same room.

Sumptuous padded headboard

you will need

Pre-cut headboard with any old coverings removed

Cordless drill with 5mm (¼in) drill bit

4oz density polyester quilting wadding: enough for a double layer across the headboard

Staple gun

Vintage fabric for the front of the headboard: enough to cover the front and just fold over onto the back

Narrow ballpoint pen

24mm (1in) diameter self-covering pronged upholstery buttons

Fabric for the back of the headboard: enough to cover the reverse of the headboard

Lace braid: enough to stick around the edge of the headboard

Hot glue gun

1 First, work out the spacing for your buttoning. Here the buttons are spaced 20cm (8in) apart and arranged in a diamond pattern. In order to do this you must first find the centre point of your headboard.

2 Working from the centre outwards, draw parallel horizontal and vertical lines every 10cm (4in). Then make a mark where lines cross, but only on alternating intersections to create the diamond effect. It is essential that your measurements are accurate, as even a slight error in the spacing will be noticeable.

3 Securing the headboard on two sturdy supports and following the manufacturer's instructions, drill a 5mm (¼in) hole through the headboard at each mark on the grid.

4 Cover the front of the headboard with two layers of the wadding, wrapping it tightly over the sides. Staple it in place on the back. The more padding you use, the more sumptuous your buttoned headboard will look when it is finished.

Continues...

Sumptuous padded headboard

5 Cut out the fabric for the front of the headboard and sew together widths if necessary. Lay it over the front of the wadding, taking the material over onto the reverse. Use the staple gun to fix the fabric in place.

6 Using the end of a narrow ballpoint pen, push it through the holes at the back of the headboard and through the wadding, and then mark and snip tiny holes in the covering fabric.

7 Cover the buttons following the manufacturer's instructions, with either the same fabric or one that complements the main colour and fabric type you are using. For each button, remove the washer then press the prong through the fabric, wadding and the hole in the back of the headboard. Slide the washer over the prongs and spread them out to hold the button in place.

8 When you are satisfied that the buttons are secure, cut out the fabric for the back of the headboard, allowing 1.5cm (⅝in) seam allowance for turning in to create a neat finish. Mark on the fabric any holes or fixings that attach the headboard to the bed, then staple the fabric to the back of the headboard.

9 To finish, stick the braid around the edge of the headboard using the hot glue gun, and reattach any fixings.

PEARLS *of* WISDOM

For your covered buttons, I suggest taking your fabric and buttons to a local haberdasher, as they have machines to make them look perfect.

I love the ottoman in my dressing room at home. An ottoman is perfect for a small space like this, because it offers both storage and somewhere to sit – and if you use a sumptuous velvet like the ottoman shown here, it will add a bit of glamour, too.

Luxury ottoman

you will need

An old ottoman with a hinged top

Cordless drill with 5mm (¼in) drill bit

4oz density polyester quilting wadding: enough for a double layer across the lid of the ottoman

Staple gun

Vintage fabric to cover the ottoman: about 3m (3yd) was used for this ottoman

Narrow ballpoint pen

14 x 24mm (1in) diameter self-covering pronged upholstery buttons

Fabric to line the underside of the ottoman

Lining fabric: enough to line the inside of the ottoman

Lace braid: enough to stick around the edge of the ottoman

Hot glue gun

1 Take the top of the ottoman from the base by unscrewing the hinges and then follow Steps 1–7 for the headboard on page 103, to create the padded lid of the ottoman.

2 You now need to cover the outside of the main body of the ottoman. With the same material that you have used on the lid, measure all around the sides of the ottoman and also its height. Add an allowance to the length for a small overlap and also add an allowance to the height for folding the fabric into the inside of the ottoman and onto the underside for attaching it. If you do not have enough material for the width, then you will need to join two pieces together, ensuring that the pattern matches up, if there is one.

3 Starting at the centre back, staple the fabric into place. Fold it over the top rim and staple on the inside and also staple it on the underside. Continue stapling along the edges, alternating top and bottom. Ensure that the fabric is pulled taut but not too tight. When you reach the centre back, ensure that one piece of the material overlaps the other and is also turned in to give a finished edge.

4 To cover the underside of the ottoman to give it a neat finish, cut the material you wish to use to the appropriate dimensions, including a 1cm (½in) seam allowance. Turning in the 1cm (½in) allowance, staple it in place.

5 Turn over the ottoman so that you are now working with it the right way up, and measure the inside of the ottoman, which will include each of the four sides and the base, again allowing for a small turn-in. Starting with the base, staple the lining material into place and then staple each side individually, again making a turn in to ensure a neat finish.

6 Attach some braid to the inside edge of the base and the inside of the lid with a hot glue gun, to cover the staples and finish. Now, finally, all you need to do is fix the lid back into place using the original or replacement screws.

Beautiful Boudoir

Now this is where you really need to get personal. Bedrooms are, perhaps more than any other room in your home, private spaces that reflect your taste and the type of style you feel most comfortable with – this is where you can really be you.

If you share your bedroom with a partner, you might need to discuss with them what kind of approach you both like – is the bedroom somewhere you find relaxing and restful, or perhaps sexy or glam? Over the years and with each house I have decorated, I think I have become increasingly bold with the design of my bedrooms. I started off with the simplest of styles – white walls and floors – and gave the room features and personality through details such as a mirrored chest of drawers and dressing table (so Marilyn Monroe), dyed lace panels and pretty cushions and bedspreads. The details are still there in my current bedroom, but now I've become more experimental with wallpaper and colour and I'm much happier with it as a statement of who I am and how I like my environment to be.

Again, the bedroom is a place where the overall design can be inspired by just one piece of furniture – a beautiful bedstead, a chest of drawers, a bedspread – anything you fall in love with and just know it has to have a place in your room. Work with that piece – if it's a focal point, tone down everything else around it; if it's quite simple, you might want to lift the room around it with patterned or colourful wallpaper, rugs, curtains and cushions. This is where you can use upcycling to your advantage; an old headboard can be given a new lease of life and identity with your favourite fabric – pretty florals or decadent velvets, or any other favourite fabric (see page 103). Simple beds or vintage iron frames can be softened or glammed up with bedspreads, throws and cushions, and four-posters look magical with lace panels draped over the top of the frame – choose the look you want and pick your pieces accordingly.

Colour schemes are down to personal choice, but most people find a bedroom a more relaxing place to be with muted colours and not too many clashing shades or patterns. You can accessorise the walls with pictures, framed objects or by hanging lace dresses to add a vintage touch, adding more or less depending on how you want the room to look – less is sometimes more on papered walls, but there's no rule.

I'm lucky enough to have a separate dressing room in my current house, but if you have wardrobes in your bedroom, make them part of the scheme too. In two of my previous homes I also had a roll-top bath in my bedroom – it made a really pretty feature, yet it could be hidden out of sight if need be with a floral-print screen. Ultimately, the bedroom is a private space, so make it the room of your dreams and let your imagination go wild.

Perfect for a child's room or for princesses of any age, an everyday mosquito net can be easily and quickly upcycled with vintage lace to create a fairytale bed canopy. I suggest that you choose a café net fabric for this canopy, as it is available in suitable lengths, which means you have a pretty top and bottom edge already made for you.

Fairytale lace canopy

you will need

Mosquito net bed canopy with support and overlay
White café net fabric with a 40cm (16in) drop (here, 3.5m/3½yd was used)
Sewing machine (optional)
2m (2yd) lace border
Ribbon or flower corsage, to finish
Hook, for hanging

1 Remove any decoration on the mosquito net (discard or add to your fabric stash) so that you are just left with the net and support.

2 Measure the circumference of the support and multiply the figure by 1.5 – this will be the length of the white café net fabric that you need.

3 Attach the net overlay to the support with a strong white cotton thread, passing the needle through the fabric and around the support. Pass the needle back through to the front of the fabric again. Continue binding the fabric and support together, gathering the fabric slightly as you work, until you have stitched all around the support. You may have some excess fabric left at the end, in which case trim it to fit so that you have a narrow overlap down the depth of the overlay. Stitch the raw edges together to finish with a running stitch (see page 208) or use a sewing machine.

4 Cut five lengths of the lace border to run from the top of the netting cone above the support to the support itself. Pin them to the mosquito net and then attach with running stitch. To hide the ends of the lace at the top, stitch on the ribbon or flower corsage.

5 Attach the canopy above the bed from a secure hook on the ceiling.

PEARLS of WISDOM

As an alternative, you could also hang lace and cotton panels over a four-poster bed. They needn't be attached; they can just hang loose.

These beautiful appliqué lace butterflies transform this soft grey satin duvet cover; such a simple but effective way to upcycle tired bed linen (or a new set). Choose whatever fabrics and appliqué motifs you like according to the style of your bedroom. This method is for a double duvet but could be easily adapted for a single.

Butterfly bed linen

you will need

Butterfly template (see page 227), or your own design

Bondaweb (fusible webbing): enough to make 2 large butterflies for the duvet cover and 1 small butterfly for each pillowcase

Complementary pieces of vintage fabric: enough to make 2 large butterflies for the duvet cover and 2 small butterflies for each pillowcase

Plain-coloured duvet cover and matching pillowcases

1 Enlarge the butterfly template on page 227 on a photocopier to the desired size (note that the image on the pillowcases is smaller) and cut out. Alternatively, draw your own bold design onto paper and cut it out to make a template.

2 Lay the template over the paper side of the Bondaweb and draw around it before roughly cutting out. Repeat for however many butterflies (or similar) you wish to appliqué onto the bedding. Lay the appliqué fabric on your ironing board, right side down, and then place the trimmed Bondaweb on top of the appliqué with the adhesive side (the 'rough' side) facing the fabric. With a medium-hot iron, press the Bondaweb onto the fabric.

3 Once cool, neatly cut out the design. Peel off the paper layer of the Bondaweb, then position each appliqué motif on the duvet cover and pillowcases (you may want to play around

with the positioning until you find the perfect combination), Bondaweb side down. Pin the butterflies to the duvet cover and pillowcases.

4 Spread the duvet cover on the ironing board. Lay a damp cloth over the top of each butterfly, then press them onto the duvet cover until they have bonded. This should only take a few seconds, but it's always good to check the manufacturer's instructions, too. Repeat with each pillowcase.

5 To finish, either leave the appliqué un-stitched or add a blanket stitch edging for decoration (see page 208).

This is a very simple patchwork quilt that uses old fabrics: small offcuts to larger pieces in gypsy-inspired, rich, jewel colours, just neatly trimmed to shape. To get the look, you want a clash of colours and a random mix of patterns and shapes. If you aren't the neatest sewer, don't worry – wobbly stitching adds to the character of the quilt.

Patchwork quilt

you will need

Assorted fabrics in various shapes and sizes: enough to make a 3m (3yd) square quilt

Sewing machine (optional)

3m (3yd) square sheet, blanket or other backing fabric

3m (3yd) square 4oz density polyester quilting wadding (optional)

Dressmaker's chalk

1 Select your fabric pieces, making sure there is a range of colours, textures and patterns. Trim the fabric to squares and rectangles of various sizes, ensuring that they add up to an area roughly 3m (3yd) square, taking into account the 5mm (¼in) seam allowance on the edge of each piece of fabric.

2 On a large surface (a clean floor may work best), lay out the fabric face down into roughly a 3m (3yd) square to create your quilt pattern. Ensure the sizes are really mixed. Play around with the layout until you are happy with the design.

3 Working from the top row, place the first two patches on top of each other, right sides facing, pin (if necessary) and hand sew using neat little running stitches (see page 208), or use a sewing machine. Stitch about 5mm (¼in) in from the edge to hem. Continue to the end of the row.

4 Repeat the method described using a jigsaw-style approach until the quilt is approximately 3m (3yd) square.

5 Spread out the patchwork on your work surface, face up, and lay the sheet, blanket or backing fabric on top, face down. Then lay the wadding on top of the sheet, blanket or backing fabric. Pin the layers together and sew around three sides, taking a 1cm (½in) seam allowance. You might choose to continue stitching by hand or now start using a sewing machine.

6 Turn the three layers right side out, so the patchwork is now on the outside and the seams are hidden. Sew the final side together using slip stitch (see page 208).

7 Working from the centre, pin the entire quilt at 20cm (8in) intervals using safety pins to hold all three layers in place. Using a long running stitch and contrasting colour of thread, hand sew rows every 20cm (8in) to quilt, if you wish. For a particularly luxurious feel, add hand-stitched patterns in a fine running stitch all over the quilt. Use dressmaker's chalk to plan your pattern. For inspiration, search for embroidered quilting patterns online.

PEARLS *of* WISDWOM

For a single bed, the measurements to aim for are 1.5 x 3m (1⅕ x 3yd).

Vintage quilts and wool blankets are fairly affordable and easy to find, and are perfect, especially ones with holes or marks, for covering old chairs. This pattern incorporates a ruffled hem in a contrasting fabric and some simple ties for the back. You only need to cut out a few pieces of fabric, so believe me – it is a lot easier than it looks.

Quilted nursing chair cover

you will need

A vintage chair with a comfortable well-padded seat and no arms
Fabric for the seat, seat sides and front back (see dimensions below)
Contrasting fabric for the back
Contrasting fabric for the ruffle
Sewing machine (optional)
Fabric or ribbons for the tie-backs: sufficient for 4 ties

1 Following the diagrams on page 118, take the following dimensions and add a 2cm (¾in) seam allowance to each one:

Seat: length (from the back to the front of the chair seat, with an extra 5cm (2in) to tuck behind the seat) x width: cut 1

Front back: length (from the top to the bottom of the back, with 5cm (2in) extra to tuck behind the seat) x width: cut 1

Seat sides: depth x length (from the outer edge of one back side round to the outer edge of the other back side): cut 1

Back sides: width (depth of back sides) x height (from the top to where the seat begins): cut 2

Back: length (from the top to the bottom of the seat sides) x two-thirds of the width of the back of the chair: cut 2

Ruffle: double the length of the seat sides x the width of the back pieces, so that you will end up with a full gather.

You may need to join several pieces of the fabric to make up the full length.

2 On each of the Back pieces, press in 5mm (¼in) and then 1cm (½in) along the overlapping sides. Stitch the hems close to the inside folded edge with a running stitch (see page 208), or use a sewing machine.

3 With right sides facing, and taking a 2cm (¾in) seam allowance, pin and then stitch together the pieces in the following order:

A: Seat sides to Seat, leaving about 7.5cm (3in) unstitched at each end.
B: Back sides to Front back, leaving about 7.5cm (3in) unstitched at each end.
C: Seat sides to Back sides.
D: Back to Back sides.

4 Turn everything right side out, and you will have the basics of the chair cover. It does not need to be a tight fit and will look presentable being a little bit on the loose side.

5 You will be left with flaps at the back of the Seat and the bottom of the Front back, which can be tucked into the chair. Finish off those edges by hemming or folding some ribbon over the edge of the fabric, and stitch in place.

Continues...

Quilted nursing chair cover

6 For the ruffle, press in 5mm (¼in) and then 1cm (½in) at each end and along the bottom edge with a loose stitch. Hem close to the inside folded edge. Gently pull the loose piece of thread at one end to make gathers. Pull up until the ruffle is the same length along the top edge as the bottom edge of the entire seat cover. With right sides facing, and taking a 2cm (¾in) seam allowance, pin and then stitch the ruffle to the cover.

7 Make two pairs of ties, with each strap about 40cm (16in) long (or cut similar lengths of ribbon), and stitch to the back pieces where they overlap. Tie the ties in a bow to secure the cover.

PEARLS *of* WISDOM

The instructions given here show you how to make a cover to fit your chair's particular measurements and can be adapted to fit any size of easy chair without arms. I have found that covers like this (and throws) are really useful for making part-furnished rental properties feel more like home.

Front view

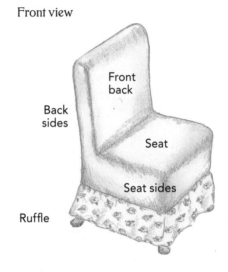

Back view

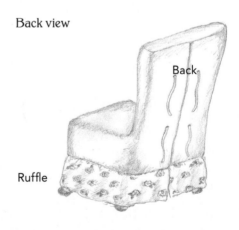

Dressing Room

Having a dressing room is a real luxury, and something I've always dreamed about, but it has taken several house moves until I've had the space to fit one in. When we moved into our current house we had a funny walk-through space next to our bedroom, which was too small to be a properly functioning room, but it makes the perfect dressing room. So, of course, that's what it became!

My favourite period is the 1920s, but the dressing room wasn't really a feature of that period, so I didn't have much inspiration to draw on when I finally got to create my version. Instead, I designed it around practicality and with my favourite look, which is probably the best starting point. Three of the walls are papered with a gorgeous vintage-inspired wallpaper featuring an antiqued English rose, and the remaining wall is covered with floor-to-ceiling wardrobes painted a deep blue.

I love seeing my clothes hanging up because they are all vintage, so I chose to have glass panels in my wardrobe doors – it lightens the room by breaking up the deep blue, but it also gives a tantalising glimpse of the beautiful vintage prints and accessories that hang behind. In previous houses I've just hung vintage dresses from rails set against the wall, which looks gorgeous, but if you worry that it looks a little temporary, you can make it look more deliberate by papering the wall behind it with your favourite print.

If you have wardrobes that are new or you don't like the way they look, you can upcycle them to suit your style. Doors look great painted or with the panels taken out and replaced with glass or even lace panels

so you get a hint of the clothes behind. If you have lots of wardrobe doors, you can soften the wall effect by adding pretty glass handles, or by hanging vintage dresses or scarves from the doors on velvet hangers (see page 130).

No lady's dressing room is complete without a dressing table, and this is the perfect spot for my favourite mirrored one. I bought it in 2001 from an antique shop in London and it has moved house with me several times – I could never part with it! Mine is original, but you can recreate the look by gluing mirrored glass to a plain table, or buy good replicas from vintage-style stores. In the middle of my room I have an ottoman, which is brilliant as somewhere to sit, and somewhere to lay out clothes. It looks lovely with a lace or a fringed shawl draped over it. A chaise longue would look good too, if you have the space. Remember that any furniture like this, including chairs, can be reupholstered with a fabric of your choice, or you can make covers for them (see page 117), or dress them up with lace. Cover the table with vintage trinkets and boxes to keep your jewellery and beauty products in, to keep the period look going.

Tailors' dummies covered in pretty floral fabrics also look gorgeous standing in a dressing room and, if you like, you can even use them for their practical purpose and hang dresses, shawls or stoles off them. You can pick these up in flea markets or even buy new ones and cover them with pretty prints.

Mirrors are of course especially useful in dressing rooms; you can make a feature of them or blend them in. If you have space, a vintage freestanding mirror can look beautiful, or you can replace a panel in a wardrobe door with a full-length piece of mirrored glass or put a mirror on the inside of the wardrobe door.

Good lighting is also important in a dressing room (it helps that you can see what you look like before you go out). I have a 1920s fringed standard lamp right next to my dressing table, but I also have the obligatory chandelier overhead. The whole look is glamorous and decadent and makes me feel like a movie star – the perfect place for enjoying a bit of that elusive me-time.

Add a little glamour to your bedroom (or any room) by upcycling a vintage-style screen. You can pick up real bargains in good condition online or at flea markets. Screens offer great solutions for modern living by hiding ugly storage or by sectioning rooms. Cover in contrasting fabrics for a bold look.

Vintage-style screen

you will need

An old screen in good working condition

Sandpaper and paint of your choice (optional) (see page 210)

Fabric to cover each panel, both front and back

Staple gun

Braid, for edging: enough to run around the edge of each panel, both front and back

Hot glue gun

1 If necessary, prepare and paint the screen (see page 210), ignoring the centre of the panels, as they are going to be covered in fabric.

2 Measure the width and height of each panel that you wish to cover and add 2cm (1in) allowance to each measurement.

3 Cut out the material and press in 1cm (½in) along each edge. Staple the fabric to the frame starting at the bottom of one panel, as close as possible to the bottom edge. Stretching the material as you go, work your way up the panel and along the top, stapling every 30cm (12in) until the front of the screen is covered. To make sure the material is taut, put further staples in the gaps to create a line of staples. Repeat for each panel, both front and back.

4 To disguise the staples, glue braid to the edges and bottom of each panel, both front and back, using the hot glue gun.

PEARLS of WISDOM

If you use a patterned material, it is important to ensure that the pattern is centred. Pay special attention and take your time. For a more sumptuous feel, stick wadding to the panels before stapling the fabric.

I picked up these old Edwardian drawers really cheaply at a local antique fair; with a bit of attention and a coat or two of my favourite chalk paint and wax, they are now fully restored and still full of character. To finish, I added cut-glass handles. The perfect finish really is all in the detail.

Upcycled chest of drawers

you will need

Chest of drawers in need of a bit of love

Sandpaper and your choice of paint (see page 210)

Dark or light wax, depending on the colour of your paint

Waxing brush

Cleaning cloth

Lint-free cloth

Wallpaper offcuts, for lining the drawers

Decorative handles

1 On a prepared work surface, remove the existing knobs of your chest of drawers and take out the drawers. Prepare all the exterior surfaces, including the drawers, and then paint them (see page 210).

2 Leave the paint to dry, then apply the wax. The easiest way to do this is with a purpose-made waxing brush, especially for the more difficult-to-reach areas. Wipe the surfaces with a cloth to remove the excess.

3 Lightly rub the paintwork and wax in places with the lint-free cloth to give a slightly aged look, and replace the drawers.

4 Line the bottom of the drawers with wallpaper, and then finally add your handles.

PEARLS *of* WISDOM

Refresh the chest of drawers every now and again with some more wax when needed, or change the look altogether with new handles and different wallpaper.

I don't like the idea of having all of my favourite items of jewellery closed away in a box or drawer, waiting for special occasions. With the exception of truly precious items I like to be able so see my necklaces, earrings, rings and bracelets. This bohemian-style shadow box is the perfect way to show them off as well as keeping them organised.

Jewellery shadow box

you will need

3cm (1¼in) deep decorative or ornate picture frame, preferably with a stand on the back and/or a hook
Foam to cover the backing board, no thicker than 5mm (¼in)
Fabric to cover the backing board
Hot glue gun
Heavy-duty picture hook (optional)
Decorative pins to hang the jewellery

1 Remove the glass from the picture frame and dispose of it safely. Remove the stiff board from the back of the picture frame, together with any tacks or tape if it is an old frame.

2 Use the board to measure and mark the foam, and cut to the same size. Lay the fabric over the board, centring the design if necessary, and also measure, mark and cut to the same size.

3 Using the hot glue gun, first stick the foam to the inside of the board and then stick the fabric onto the foam.

4 Put the board back into the frame and secure with the existing tacks. Hang the frame from a picture hook or sit it on the top of a dressing table. Add the decorative pins and your favourite pieces of jewellery to finish.

PEARLS *of* WISDOM

You could also use a hinged shadow box for more precious jewellery, following the method as above but replacing the glass at the end. You could even attach a small latch to the door and lock with a small padlock.

Add a bit of elegance to an everyday item with this simple velvet coat hanger. Padded hangers are great for hanging vintage dresses over mirrors or doors, adding a romantic touch to bedrooms and dressing rooms.

Velvet padded coat hangers

you will need

1m x 2.5cm (1yd x 1in) ribbon
Wooden coat hanger
Double-sided tape
Fabric offcuts (I have used velvet): enough to cover the hanger
4oz weight polyester quilting wadding: enough to cover the hanger
2 pins with decorative pearl heads

1 Cut a length of ribbon sufficient to cover the hook of the hanger (about 50cm/20in) and stick a length of double-sided tape on one side. Starting at the tip of the hook, tightly wind the ribbon around the hook until it is all covered, finishing where the hook goes into the hanger.

2 Measure the height of the wooden part of the coat hanger and multiply by four. Measure the length of the wooden part of the coat hanger and add 2cm (¾in). Mark out these measurements on the fabric and wadding and cut out. Cut a slit in the centre of one long edge of both pieces of material to reach the middle (see diagram opposite).

3 Lay the wadding on your work surface and stick strips of double-sided tape along the top and bottom edges. Position the hanger in the centre of the fabric so that the amount of fabric that lies at the bottom equals the depth of the hanger. Then fold up the bottom edge

of the wadding and stick it to the top edge of the hanger. Fold down the top edges of the wadding on either side of the hook, wrap it right around the hanger and stick it to the back of it at the top. Tuck in the excess fabric at each end and use slip stitches (see page 208) to close.

4 Repeat Step 3 with the covering fabric, but this time, don't stick double-sided tape along the top edge. Wrap the fabric around the hanger as before, but for the back seam, fold under 1cm (½in) and slip stitch in place. Stitch the ends together.

5 With the remaining ribbon, make a large bow and stitch it to the cover where the hook goes into the hanger.

6 To finish, add the pearl-headed pins to the top of the hanger, to hold up your dresses if need be.

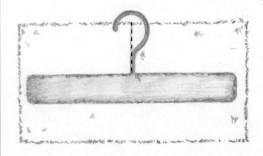

Lavender hearts not only smell heavenly but can also be decorative if made with beautiful fabrics and embellished with lace, beads or velvet ribbon. A simpler variation is to use scraps of vintage fabric for the heart and not worry about the lace layer.

Lavender & lace heart

you will need

Vintage velvet fabric
Lace offcut
Heart template (see page 229)
Dressmaker's chalk
Lace or velvet ribbon for each heart, to hang
Small amount of polyester stuffing
Small amount of dried lavender
Diamanté beads and buttons, to finish

1 Lay the fabric and lace on your work surface, right sides down. Photocopy the template on page 229, cut it out and then draw around it twice on both the fabric and lace using dressmaker's chalk. Cut out the heart shapes.

2 Fold the ribbon in half, right sides out. Lay the hearts and ribbon loop on top of each other in the following order:

> **Velvet** heart (right side up)
> **Lace** heart
> **Ribbon** loop with the loop in the 'V' at the top and the ends pointing towards the bottom of the heart
> **Lace** heart
> **Velvet** heart (right side down).

Ensure all edges are aligned and pin together.

3 Sew the layers together with a small running stitch, leaving a 1cm (½in) seam allowance (taking care to ensure the ribbon ends aren't caught in the stitching). Stop about 2.5cm (1in) before you reach the end. Trim the seam and turn the heart right side out.

4 Insert plenty of stuffing and lavender so the heart is full and rounded, and slip stitch the gap closed (see page 208). To personalise, stitch on some diamanté beads and/or buttons.

Art Deco

For me, mirrored Art Deco furniture is what my vintage style is all about. My love affair with this style of furniture started in 1996 when I was walking through Camden Market in London with Danny and my eldest daughter Daisy, when in a corner of one of the stalls I spotted a mirrored 1920s bar.

It was possibly one of the most beautiful and decadent things I had ever seen, and unfortunately it was not only completely out of our price range, but we also had nowhere to put it. However, in 2000 I was passing another market when I noticed a gorgeous mirrored chest of drawers. It was simply stunning. Being the impulsive person that I am, I went in and asked if I could buy it and get it delivered that day. It was, and it has remained, one of my favourite pieces of furniture that I have ever owned. In fact, my love for mirrored furniture has continued, as I have since bought a gorgeous 1920s dressing table from an antique shop as well as a side table on eBay and a sweet jewellery box that I found in a local junk shop.

The Art Deco movement originated in Europe – most popularly in Paris – in around 1908, but really took hold after the First World War and dominated as THE style until just before the outbreak of the Second World War. In the 1950s, the furniture became increasingly popular again when celebrities like Marilyn Monroe were photographed with pieces in their homes. Hollywood caught the bug, and soon mirrored furniture was appearing on sets on television and on the big screen. By the 1980s, the popularity of this type of furniture had decreased, mainly because of the low-quality mirrors that manufacturers were using, but since then this has changed and the style has been enjoying a revival.

The style just oozes glamour and aspirational living. Angular, geometric furniture was made from chrome, glass and mirror tiles, or using rich woods patterned with motifs (particularly sunburst ones)

or inlaid with exotic materials such as ebony. Art Deco is an indulgent style that is all about elegance and drama and less about practicality – and it is gorgeous.

Authentic mirrored Art Deco pieces can be pricey, as they are becoming increasingly rare and so harder to get hold of. Equally, however, they do hold their value well so they are a good investment; if you can afford a piece – and you take good care of it – you can sometimes even make a profit. Fortunately, because this furniture is carefully and meticulously crafted and each piece demands your attention, you only need one or two pieces in one room. If the originals are a little out of your price range, then you can find lots of reproductions in vintage-style homeware stores. If these are still too expensive for you, try getting an old chest of drawers and covering it in pieces of mirror. I did this in my mint-green 1950s caravan and it looked unbelievably authentic. I have also covered an old coffee table in mirror and everyone who saw it was quite shocked that it wasn't an original.

Mirrored furniture comes in a variety of styles that are suitable for the living room, bedroom and even the bathroom. Using this furniture to decorate your home is a wonderful way of bringing elegance and sophistication to the plainest of rooms. For the best impact, though, keep everything around the furniture simple; mirrored pieces in particular look best in white rooms, although if you do want colour, floral wallpapers are fine; keep patterns small, though, and colours knocked back so they don't draw the eye away. Popular colours of the time were creams, pale greens, beige and oyster to emphasise the dark wood and chrome, but because there was also a real craze for travel in the early 20th century – which meant animal skins and mother-of-pearl were really popular – Art Deco furniture looks great with leopard and other safari prints. In my bedroom I have a leopard-print chair at my mirrored dressing table, whereas in a previous bedroom I let my mirrored furniture steal the show, setting it against white-painted walls and a wooden floor with only grey lace curtains and a silvery grey bedspread to break up the white look.

This furniture was originally designed to sit against polished wooden parquet floors or black and white tiles, but if you really must have carpet, go for as neutral a colour as possible, or get an original Art Deco rug or replica style, or perhaps go for a shaggy pale rug. As with everything else, stick to simple, unfussy lighting; keep lamps to a minimum and go for less dramatic chandeliers and lampshades – although 1920s fringed shades always look great.

I often get bored with furniture and sell it on, but I can honestly say that I'd like to pass down my mirrored Art Deco furniture pieces to my children, and I won't be selling them any time soon.

Vinyl ceiling rose

This simple idea using self-adhesive vinyl is an affordable way to enhance lampshades or chandeliers. You can also make small self-adhesive vinyl wall decorations.

you will need

Ceiling rose template (see page 228), or your own design

Self-adhesive matt vinyl

Craft knife

Cutting mat

Soft cloth

1 Enlarge the template on page 228 on a photocopier to the desired size and cut out two copies. If you are designing your own template, I recommend splitting it into two halves, like the one in this book, and making sure that you leave enough room in the centre for the light fitting.

2 Lay the vinyl face down on your work surface and draw around the template. Carefully cut out the shape using the craft knife on a cutting mat.

3 Before applying the vinyl to the ceiling, make sure the surface is free from grease and completely dry. Then gently peel the backing off the vinyl and carefully place the sticker in the correct position, lightly sticking down the edges first. Once the vinyl is stuck to the ceiling, it can be moved, but only slightly. You may need an extra pair of hands to help here.

4 Using a soft cloth, wipe over the vinyl to remove any air bubbles, starting at the middle and moving out to the edges.

Bird wall stickers

you will need

Bird template (see page 229)
Self-adhesive matt vinyl
Craft knife
Cutting mat
Pencil
Spirit level
Soft cloth

1 Photocopy the template on page 229, resize if desired and cut it out. If you are using your own design, draw it on some paper and cut it out. When choosing the ideal place for your wall art, place the design against the wall to get a feel for the height and spacing.

2 Lay the vinyl face down on your work surface and draw around the template. Very carefully cut out the shape using the craft knife and cutting mat.

3 Before applying the vinyl to the wall, make sure the surface is free from grease and completely dry; non-textured surfaces are best. Mark the wall with a pencil where you want to stick the shapes, using a spirit level if necessary.

4 Gently peel the backing off the vinyl and carefully place the sticker in the correct position. Lightly stick the edges down first to ensure it is accurately positioned. Once the vinyl is stuck to the wall, it can be moved, but only slightly.

5 Using a soft cloth, wipe over the vinyl to remove any air bubbles, starting at the middle and moving to the outer edges.

Vintage Child's Room

I 've always loved decorating my kids' rooms. When they were much younger I could really go to town and create something magical for them, but even now that they have an opinion and their own style, they still like the uniqueness that they get from a vintage look.

The sex of your child is key to the design of a room. When they are babies, you can get away with a more feminine feel, but as boys in particular get bigger they are not so keen on lots of lace and pastel colours! When my boys were small, I decorated their room in white – white walls, white floorboards, white ceiling, and I even painted matching old antique iron hospital beds white. To introduce some warmth to the scheme, I dyed lace panels royal blue for their windows and painted their chandelier the same colour to match. It looked ever so sweet. I did the same for my daughter Daisy's room, but using a shocking pink dye for the lace curtain and pink glass paint for the chandelier.

Since then I've discovered wallpaper, which makes a great alternative to paint. The boys' rooms don't have wallpaper on the walls, just bright paint, but I have papered the ceiling with a star wallpaper, which makes it really cosy. I've also painted their wardrobe doors too to add further interest to the room.

Colour aside, the other crucial element in any child's room is storage. Kids are messy, let's face it, and they have a lot of stuff, which changes as they grow up. When they were younger I lined shelves with cheap baskets that I spray painted in fun colours, so I could just scoop up their toys at the end of the day and get them out of the way and out of sight. Wardrobes are good too, not only for clothes but also for hiding storage boxes. I've collected antique fairy costumes and dresses

over the years, which I hang on wardrobes around the room, and they looked especially pretty in the girls' rooms – before they became tomboys!

I've always enjoyed finding little trinkets to make the children's rooms look original and give them personality; in particular antique dolls, teddy bears and old pictures to add to the vintage look. I have a real passion for cabinets, too, which I paint or decorate with pretty handles or fabric panels. Depending on their size they are great for storing books, notepads, trinkets and other bits and bobs, and they will last a long time as they will always be useful, even as the child gets older and needs somewhere to store different things. You can also update their look as the child forms his or her own personality and style by simply painting them again.

As they get to a certain age, kids need a workspace; girls love dressing tables when they are young to play dressing up, but then they double up well as desks for homework later on. My new obsession is old writing desks. Victorian ones are a particular passion of mine, and they are great to paint and put vintage fabric inside. You can make new or vintage desks fit into the décor or create a focal point – whichever you prefer – by painting them white in a coloured room, or in a vibrant colour in a white room. Chairs are a must for a child's bedroom, whether to set at a desk or a dressing table, or simply just as a feature in the room. In the house we're in now, I've collected vintage children's chairs in all different colours and styles and an antique distressed table for my daughter Betty and her friends to sit at. Chairs also look great with a vintage cushion or toy on them.

The key thing to decorating a child's room in a vintage style is, of course, safety. If old furniture is damaged or splintered, a child's room is probably not the best place for it, unless you can sand down the rough bits. If something is delicate, too, it won't last five minutes in a small child's room, so you are better off saving yourself the heartache of seeing a beautiful thing ruined by finding another home for it or giving it to them when they are old enough to look after it.

Nº 4

Bathrooms
&
Small and Special
Spaces

I love mirrors with a distressed finish. With this project you don't have to wait years or spend lots of money on an antique to get the look. It does involve some strong acid, though, so please wear your mask and goggles and work in a ventilated area – outside is best. If you can, use an older mirror, as the process is slightly easier.

Antique ghost mirror

you will need

Old mirror without a backing (or with an easily removable backing), for access to the back of the glass
Protective sheet
Safety goggles or glasses
Face mask
Heavy-duty chemical-resistant rubber gloves
Paint stripper
Stencil brush
Paper towels
Hydrochloric acid, in a spray bottle for safety

1 In a room with very good ventilation (preferably outside) and plenty of room to move around, lay out a thick protective sheet on your work surface. Put on the goggles, face mask and gloves, wear a long-sleeved top and follow all other safety instructions provided by the manufacturer.

2 Place the mirror face down on the work surface. Then generously spray or paint (depending on the brand you purchase) the glass with paint stripper. Leave it to stand for about 30 minutes until the paint backing can be easily moved around or removed with the stencil brush.

3 Using paper towels, wipe the stripper off the mirror, then wash it with soapy water. Wipe once more with kitchen towels and then spray the hydrochloric acid randomly onto the back of the mirror. Leave it to stand for about 20 minutes, which should give plenty of time for the acid to take effect.

4 Using the stencil brush, move the loose 'silver' around as if you were stirring it to create the mottled effect. Leave the mirror overnight to dry. Dispose of any excess acid and the equipment that you have used with the acid in accordance with the manufacturer's guidelines.

PEARLS *of* WISDOM

You can also scrape off the loosened silver or shuffle it around to give a crackled effect, or paint on some gold or silver paint (or any colour you wish, but it needs to be dark to work well).

Crates are fantastically versatile, really inexpensive and easy to source. They come in all shapes and sizes, vintage and new, and can have many uses around the home, from bedside tables to shelving and general storage. Here a single crate is transformed into a bathroom cabinet.

Mini bathroom cabinet

you will need

Old wine crate

2 MDF shelves, one for the centre of the crate and the other for the bottom, to give a flat base

Cordless drill

8 L-shaped brackets

Softwood timber, cut to fit the open front of the crate

Screws for the door, shelves and wall mounting

Screwdriver

Sandpaper and paints of your choice (see page 210)

Lace or fabric, for the door

Staple gun

Braid, for the door

Hot glue gun

Hinges

Clasp and hook

Pretty door handle (optional)

1 On a prepared work surface and with the crate standing on one end, decide where the shelves are to be placed. Measure from front to back and from side to side. You need to take measurements for both shelves and where they are to be fixed as the crate may not be square.

2 Either cut the shelves yourself out of MDF, or ask a professional to do this for you. In each corner of the back of the crate, following the manufacturer's guidelines, drill a hole so that when you have finished you will be able to wall mount the cabinet if you wish.

3 Mark where the shelf brackets are to be fixed, ensuring these are level, and then drill the holes.

4 Still with the crate upright, measure the height for two of the pieces of the softwood timber for the door frame. Then measure the width for the other two pieces and buy them cut to size, or saw them carefully yourself. Place the two pieces of wood for the width at the top and bottom of the wood you have cut for the height. Check they are at right angles and then screw together.

5 Prepare and paint the whole of the crate, both inside and outside, together with the shelves and door (see page 210).

6 When the paint has dried, attach the shelving brackets and place the shelves inside.

7 Measure around the inside of the door and cut the lace or fabric to fit, adding 1cm (½in) to turn under for a neat finish. Press under the excess fabric with an iron and then staple the fabric to the inside of the door. So that you can't see the staples and for a more polished finish, stick braid over the top with a hot glue gun.

8 Attach the hinges to the door and then to the crate. They can be on either the left-hand or right-hand side – it's your choice. On the opposite side to the hinges attach the clasp and hook.

9 Finally, attach a small door handle. Bear in mind the length of the screw, as the door is not very thick.

Heavenly Bathrooms

For me, a bathroom has two roles (beyond the obvious practical function): it needs to be at times cosy and at times glamorous.

In this room, perhaps more than any other, the colour scheme is definitely the most important element in creating your vintage style. That should be your first decision, and the rest of the design will form around it. You might like to keep the walls and floors in monochrome colours – perhaps even both the same colour – or you might prefer a bright blend of colours. Although I love wallpaper, this is one room where it doesn't really work – the obvious presence of water means that it will get steamed off or marked. (Ditto for any pictures on the wall – they're best avoided, but if you do hang pictures, make sure they aren't precious and irreplaceable.)

If you want to add a splash of colour here and there, paint or tile the bath panel (if there is one), tile around a bath or shower, or use blinds or lace curtains. Vintage tiles are hard to find in any great quantity, but if you can find a few random ones you can set them among white or coloured tiles to add splashes of pattern in a plain space, or you can make your own (see page 18). If you have cupboards or shelves in your bathroom, paint these in various shades of your favourite colours, either as a unified scheme or as a bright clash of colours. This is particularly worth doing if you buy an old piece of furniture that needs rescuing, or a modern piece that looks too new and soulless. Choose your towels carefully too – these can become focal points in a room, so pick colours that work with the room, or indulge in patterns or floral themes that you can't get on the walls with paper.

I have a passion for roll-top baths. You don't have to have a large room to have a roll-top bath, as they come in many different sizes. You

can get modern replicas of these in all shapes and styles, but they are pricey. I buy all mine off eBay, where they are both cheap and the real thing. They may have the odd mark or chip, but I think this just adds to the romance of them. Although I'd say love what you buy, you need to think practically a bit too. Lost in the romance of the style, I once bought a slipper bath, adoring the shape and curves of it, but sadly it proved to be uncomfortable and not at all relaxing to be in! So if you can, try before you buy. Taps, sinks and other details can be found on eBay, too, or have a rummage through your nearest reclamation yard.

As a working mother, to me the bathroom is my sanctuary, a place where I can retreat and relax after a long day. As in any room in the house, lighting is important here to create a mood. I don't want to be reclining in the bath with bright lights glaring, but equally, low-level lights such as lamps are a no-no in bathrooms for safety reasons. So to achieve a cosy, restful atmosphere I like to scatter scented candles around the room, and although people say you can't have chandeliers in bathrooms – I do. You can't beat a bit of glamour!

Mirrors have a practical place in a bathroom and they look beautiful – and can also make a small room look bigger. There are so many beautiful mirrors out there, both genuine vintage or vintage-style, and this is where the choice really comes down to what you like. You can go small and pretty, or large to make a statement; it's all about what you fall in love with and how much wall space you have to give it. Indeed, you can even create your own vintage-style mirror (see page 148). One piece of advice I do have for buying mirrors is that, as with everything vintage, if you see an antique piece that's right for your home, buy it there and then, as you may never see anything like it again.

Storage in a bathroom is a must – whether for toiletries or towels – but again, choose pieces that work with the style. Painted shelves with baskets look cosy; painted chests (I'm really into the vintage Italian-style gold-painted ones) look glam. Like everything in a bathroom, love it but also make sure it's fit for purpose, and you can't go wrong.

Gold-dipped bathroom accessories

This spray-painted glassware will instantly give your bathroom a touch of 1920s glamour. I have used cut glass because the spray paint highlights the design, but you could use metal or ceramics. And you don't have to use gold. You could use any colour you wish.

you will need

Soap dish, liquid soap dispenser, glass goblet for toothbrushes, any other bathroom accessories

Masking tape

Gold spray paint for wood, metal, glass and ceramics

Disposable gloves (optional)

1 On a prepared work surface select your first item and apply masking tape to the area(s) that you want to remain untouched. Remember that spray paint disperses over a wide area, so you will need to completely cover the rest of the item to avoid unwanted spray marks.

2 Stand about 25cm (10in) from the object and apply the spray paint. Leave to dry for about 8 hours. Always wash by hand.

PEARLS *of* WISDOM

You could add embellishments such as diamanté beads or tassels.

Homemade candles

As well as soft lighting and a sense of tranquillity, scented candles give a home a signature smell. A few years ago a friend introduced me to wonderful all-natural soy candles. Made from soybeans, these candles burn cleaner and longer than the more traditional paraffin-based ones, perfect for a relaxing bath.

you will need

Double boiler or a large pan for the water and a smaller pan to sit inside to melt the wax flakes

450g (1lb) soy candle wax flakes, which makes 3–5 candles

1 x 2cm (½ x ¾in) coloured wax chip per candle

4 tbsp candle-making fragrance oil

Cooking thermometer

Glass or vintage candleholders (see pearls of wisdom, below)

Waxed wicks with holders

Chopsticks, pencils or cutlery

1 Protect your work surface with lots of newspaper. Soy candlewax is easily removed with warm soapy water, but it is better to be prepared.

2 Pour water into the bottom portion of a double boiler and bring it to the boil. Then put the wax flakes in the top part of the double boiler. Reduce the heat to low, and as the wax reaches 175–185°C (347–365°F) it will start to melt.

3 As the wax melts, start adding the coloured wax chips. Wax always becomes paler as it cools, so you may need to add more dye, depending on how you want your candle to look. You may find that you need a few attempts to get the colour right.

4 Remove the double boiler from the heat and add your fragrance oil – I use roughly 4 tbsp per 450g (1lb) of wax, but also check the manufacturer's instructions. Using too much could disrupt the flame or create greasy spots on the candle.

5 Making sure that you keep stirring the wax, let it cool to around 140°C (285°F) – this is where the cooking thermometer comes in handy. At the same time, heat the candleholders in a low oven to warm them up,

which will prevent cracking when the wax is poured into them. Once they are warm and the wax is at the right temperature, pour the wax into your containers.

6 Put a wick (with its metal holder) in each container and keep each wick upright by supporting it between four chopsticks placed in a grid around the wick. You could also use straws, pencils or some cutlery as supports.

7 If you are placing a lid on the container, let the wax cool completely before covering the candle. In most cases the candle will need to set overnight before it can be lit.

8 If any air bubbles have formed or any frosting (where the wax goes white and patchy) appears on the top of the wax, use a hair dryer to even out the top.

9 Before lighting your candle you need to make sure the wax is at room temperature. Trim the wick to 1.5cm (⅝in) above the top of the candle, then light it.

PEARLS *of* WISDOM

If you are planning on giving the candle as a gift, consider using a container that can be reused after the candle has been spent – a teacup or pretty glass dish would be perfect. Trim wicks regularly to prevent them from smoking and to get the best burning results.

Creative
Walls

D ue to my obsession with wallpaper, few walls in our house get left
plain. And if they do, they won't stay that way for long, as I can
usually use them as a backdrop for pictures, tapestries or other
interesting or quirky wall hangings.

Walls are the ideal spots for displaying vintage pieces, and generally
these are things that can be bought inexpensively at flea markets and in
junk shops. Frames, little cabinets or antique wall lights can really add
personality to a wall and give the finishing touches to a room.

Anything can be framed; you don't just have to restrict it to photos
or pictures: bits of lace – an antique collar or a cuff – tapestries or even
some of the kids' special pieces of artwork. We found a Union Jack flag
from the First World War in a junk shop, which was slightly torn, but
we framed it and it looks wonderful; you can barely see the damage.
And I once made an anniversary present for Danny out of old buttons
in the shape of a heart and displayed it in an old frame. Also look for
interesting pieces of art; I have a taxidermy-inspired feather and flower
wreath that I bought from a local gallery.

You can get hold of old tapestries in markets and junk shops, and
many are lovely and have a real sense of history. Framed tapestries
tend to be more expensive than unframed ones, so go for the latter if
you can, and then you can look around for a nice vintage frame to put
it in. Framed tapestries look particularly good against wallpaper, but
wherever you put them, don't hang them in bright sunlight or the colour
of the threads will start to fade. A friend of mine has lots of antique
mirrors all over the wall in her dining room; it makes a room look a
lot bigger.

You can get vintage frames from all the usual places. Some may
have damage or be missing glass, but often these can be repaired
by you or a specialist; if it's a really beautiful and unique frame it'll
be worth the expense. You can also buy cheap modern frames and

upcycle them with distressed paint techniques or coloured paint. Gold frames look really dramatic against dark patterned wallpaper. Photos on modern canvas blocks can be made to blend into a vintage scheme by wrapping lace around the edges to soften their appearance. When grouping frames on a wall, try to avoid a unified look of one size, colour or shape; mix and match them so that they all stand out from one another and don't get lost.

One of my other vintage obsessions is little cabinets and curiosity display cases – I can't get enough of them. Old ones in good condition can be pricey, but they are worth it. Again, if they are a little damaged, or you want to upcycle a modern copy, you can paint the outsides or line the insides with a small-print floral wallpaper. These can then be hung anywhere – in kitchens, bathrooms, living rooms and bedrooms – where they can serve an aesthetic purpose as well as providing a practical storage or display solution.

I also love hanging arrangements of twigs or feathers on the wall. I bought mine from a local artisan market but you can get lots of modern versions from home fairs or online, or if you want to make them, there are plenty of attractive ideas you can research online, too. Lots of places sell these kinds of decorations at Christmas, but if you choose natural-looking hearts or stars without glitter or Christmas touches, they can look good all year round. If you like, you can accessorise them with a bit of ribbon or a piece of lace, too. Of course, at Christmas they are also brilliant for hanging little vintage decorations on.

Feathers look amazing in arrangements, and I have a beautiful circular one on my door, which is really glamorous and elegant. Heart-shaped lavender bags made from floral prints or lace (see page 133) look pretty hanging from handles on doors, cupboards or wardrobes, or even from hooks on walls or vintage light fittings, which can make interesting focal points in their own right.

On walls, anything goes. If you have a trinket, a photo or some other cherished thing, hang it up, frame it or give it pride of place on a shelf. Don't be afraid to make a feature of something personal and special to you.

I absolutely adore vintage china, but more often than not it sits in a cupboard out of view and only comes out on very special occasions. Sourcing beautiful mismatched plates to create a feature display on a wall will make the most of pretty designs. Here's how to add your own bespoke touch.

Decorative china plates

you will need

Royalty- or copyright-free image(s) (see page 230), or a design of your own to fit the plates

A4 inkjet waterslide transfer paper

Inkjet printer (it must be inkjet; this process isn't compatible with a laserjet printer)

Old china plates

D-cut squeegee

1 Select your image and print it onto the waterslide transfer paper using an inkjet printer and following the manufacturer's instructions. Remember that the image will ultimately be reversed, so don't choose a picture that will look odd when it's back to front; for example, images that contain words or numbers. If you are creating your own design, you will need to scan it in to your computer first.

2 Put the printed design into a bowl of warm water and wait for 60 seconds until the design can be removed from the backing paper.

3 On a prepared work surface, slip the design from the backing paper onto the plate and use the squeegee to make it smooth. Wash away any gum from the surface of the design with a clean damp sponge. Leave the plate to dry at room temperature for 8–10 hours.

4 Preheat the oven to 140°C (275°F/Gas mark 1). Put the plate in the oven for 10–20 minutes to seal the transfer. When the image turns shiny, as if glazed, it is ready. Turn off the oven and allow the plate to cool before taking it out to cool completely.

Inexpensive little side tables can be picked up at most secondhand shops, and one of the reasons I love them so much is because they can sit snugly into even the smallest corner of a room or hallway. Be bold with colour and finishes – the look is all in the detail.

Opulent gold occasional table

you will need

Small side table

Sandpaper and undercoat (see page 210)

Gold spray paint or gold paint

Lace or fabric, slightly larger than the table top

Dressmaker's chalk

Staple gun

Braid for edging

Hot glue gun

1 Prepare and paint the table with undercoat (see page 210). When it has dried, apply the gold spray paint or gold paint to the table on a protected work surface. Follow the manufacturer's instructions and watch out for drips.

2 Leave the table to dry overnight, or for at least 5 hours.

3 Lay the fabric you are using for the table top on your work surface, right side down. Turn the table upside down and stand it in the middle of the fabric. Measure the depth of the table top and then draw around the edge of the table with dressmaker's chalk, adding the depth as an allowance.

4 Cut out the fabric, lay it over the top of the table and then staple it all around the edge on the lip of the top, keeping the fabric taut.

5 Finish off the table by sticking braid around the edge using the hot glue gun, to cover the staples.

Vintage suitcase storage

I am always looking for different and decorative storage ideas. Old suitcases and trunks are perfect for this. You can find a range online, at flea markets and in secondhand shops, from large leather suitcases to detailed vanity cases. A collection of vintage cases stacked in descending size order can make an interesting feature.

you will need

Old suitcase or trunk
Soft cleaning cloth
Fabric: large enough to line the inside of the lid and the case
Braid or lace trim: enough to run around the edge of the inside of the lid and the rim of the case
Hot glue gun

1 Give the suitcase a good clean using a soft cloth. To make the lining for the inside of the suitcase, measure the base and sides and mark the dimensions on a single piece of fabric as one complete shape; it should resemble a rough cross. Repeat the process using the dimension for the lid.

2 Stick the fabric lining to the inside of the suitcase and the lid using the hot glue gun. Work section by section and bear in mind that the glue coming off the gun cools down very quickly.

3 Cut the braid or trim into appropriate lengths to line the inner edges of the suitcase and lid. Stick it in place with the glue gun. Your suitcase is now ready to store all your favourite bits and bobs.

PEARLS *of* WISDOM

If the outside of your suitcase or trunk is a little the worse for wear, consider spray painting it to cover up the blemishes.

Vintage wine crates make excellent storage containers and can be easily transformed with a little attention. Here, chalky pastel shades and a floral stencil complete the look. Pick your colours and stencil design to complement your room; you could even create a set, or stencil on your initials.

Stencilled storage crate

you will need

Old crate
Sandpaper and paints of your choice (see page 210)
Stencil outline (see page 224)
Cutting mat
A4 sheet of transparent acetate
Masking tape
Craft knife
Stippling brush

1 Prepare and paint the crate all over, both inside and out (see page 210).

2 Once the paint has dried you can apply the stencil. If you are using a design from this book, photocopy it, enlarging if necessary. If you are making your own design, simply draw it on some paper. Lay the design on the cutting mat and then lay the acetate over the top and secure it in place with some masking tape.

3 Using a sharp craft knife, begin cutting along the longest, straightest edges of the stencil design, as these are the easiest. Try to cut each line only once, so make sure you press firmly and smoothly. Use your free hand to secure the acetate and image, but make sure you keep your fingers well away from where you are cutting. As you are cutting, turn the cutting mat so you are always cutting at an easy angle and away from you as much as possible. Once you have cut out the whole design, tidy up any rough edges (so paint doesn't get caught up in these), and your stencil is ready to use.

4 Attach the stencil to the crate with the masking tape, and use the paint-loaded stippling brush in a rocking motion to transfer the design to the crate, through the stencil. It's fun to experiment, although you might prefer to practice on some paper before stencilling on the crate.

5 Leave the crate to dry for 4–5 hours and then fill it with your favourite cushions, blankets and linens.

PEARLS of WISDOM

This stencil would also look really pretty on sanded stairs or a door.

Cosy Corners

In a family home it's great to have a playroom where the kids can go and get out all their toys and play without getting under everyone else's feet, but there are other times when it's really nice to spend some chill-out time together as a family. I love the idea of a snug, or a family room – a space that is cosy and warm and where we can all relax together, play cards or board games, watch the television or talk about the day's events. It's a grown-up retreat that we can all enjoy.

Traditionally a snug is a small room that is somewhere cosy in the winter, but of course it has year-round appeal. Whether summer or winter, the best way to keep a room cosy is to go with a style that feels warm and relaxing. For this, the best colours are warm reds, terracotta and gold, and this is a room where wallpaper works really well, too, particularly darker ones with large floral prints. Wooden floors stained or painted in dark colours are best for a sense of warmth, and you can soften them with shaggy sheepskin rugs or other big rugs if you like. Of course, rules are made to be broken, and if you feel more relaxed in a bright space, go for lighter colours all over.

Seating is key: big L-shaped sofas or even a chaise longue work really well and look inviting with shawls and throws draped over them and deep-coloured velvet or tapestry cushions scattered around. Again, darker fabrics look good here, or even leather cushions on sofas, and big curtains or darker lace panels at the window create an intimate space. Pick side tables made of darker wood and put pretty fringed lamps on top of them, and also add light with mirrored boxes or glass trinkets.

A snug makes a fantastic retreat for reading in, so line a wall with bookshelves filled with books, or even DVDs, and get yourself a big armchair to curl up in, perhaps draped with lace or faux fur. You need good light for reading, but a snug really demands gentle, low-level lighting, so use table-top lamps around the room and perhaps position a standard lamp near the armchair. Of course, a coloured chandelier would also look lovely, as would some fairy lights along the mantelpiece or wound around curtain poles.

I'm a big fan of scented candles; they really add to the ambience of a room, and in a snug they can create a cosy feel with their calming fragrance and flickering light. If you have a chimney, this is the ideal space for a real fire or a log burner, as they will give the room instant character. You can get beautiful antique fireplace surrounds and mantelpieces from reclamation yards, as well as fabulous old grates. Mirrors look attractive over mantelpieces and also reflect light into the room, or a colourful big picture can set the tone. I love to put vintage candlesticks and quirky trinkets on the mantelpiece as well as scented candles and old clocks. Big baskets look wonderful in front of a fireplace for storing wood, as well as elsewhere around the room to keep newspapers and magazines out of the way.

This is a family space, for relaxing rather than entertaining, so the key thing is to keep it simple and personal; ultimately it should feel like a space in which you can unwind and feel completely at home. Bliss!

Screen-printed floral wallpaper

The stencil method for screen-printing is a great way to create something truly unique for your home. You can incorporate your bespoke designs onto fabric for curtains or bedding, for example, or make wrapping paper, thank-you cards and even wallpaper. You can make it as intricate and complicated as you like, as in the picture, but for your first attempt stick to bold graphic motifs and a single colour.

you will need

Rose and leaves stencil (see pages 232–3)

Cutting mat

Screen-printing kit complete with screen, acetate, ink and a squeegee

Masking tape

Craft knife

Roll of lining paper

Ready-mixed screen-printing ink, if you want a different colour to the one supplied in the kit

1 If you are using the design from this book, photocopy the rose stencil on pages 232–3 (enlarging if desired). If you are making your own design, simply draw it on some paper. Lay the design on the cutting mat, lay the acetate from the stencil kit over the top and secure it in place with some masking tape. If you are using your own acetate, ensure that it is the same size as the screen-printing frame or else the ink will leak around the sides of the acetate.

2 Using a sharp craft knife, begin cutting along the longest, straightest edges of the stencil design, as these are the easiest. Try to cut each line only once, so make sure you press firmly and smoothly.

Continues...

Screen-printed floral wallpaper

Use your free hand to secure the acetate and image, but make sure you keep your fingers well away from where you are cutting. As you are cutting, turn the cutting mat so you are always cutting at an easy angle and away from you as much as possible.

3 Once you have cut out the whole design, tidy up any rough edges (so paint doesn't get caught up in these), and your stencil is ready to use.

4 Stick the stencil to the side of the screen-printing frame that will rest on the wallpaper – the flat side. Stick masking tape along each side of the stencil outline. If there is a right and wrong way to the design, make sure it is taped to the frame back to front.

5 Unroll the lining paper, and lay the screen-printing frame on it where you want the design to be. Pour a tablespoon of screen-printing ink in a line along the top edge of the screen and, using the squeegee, push the ink across the screen without applying too much pressure. Then, holding the screen firmly with one hand, pull the squeegee down the screen, this time applying some pressure, taking the ink with it. Repeat, and then put the squeegee to one side, being careful not to drip any excess ink.

6 Holding the lining paper down with one hand, lift the screen up from the bottom edge and then away. Depending on how successful you have been, you might want to treat this as a test run.

7 To make wallpaper, repeat Steps 5 and 6 across the roll, lining up the pattern carefully to ensure a regular pattern.

8 For a two-colour design, once your first layer is dry repeat the process with a second stencil (see pages 232–3 for the leaves template if you are following the design in this book) positioning the screen-printing frame each time to line up with the initial design.

9 When you have finished, remove the stencil and wash all the ink off the screen.

the
OPTIONS
ARE AS
endless
as your
imagination

Nº5

Opulent

Office

✝

If you are short on space this slightly mad idea will help you store all your paperwork, files and stationery and also offers a compact working space – and when you are done you can just close the door and hide it all away. Affordable secondhand wardrobes of all shapes, styles and sizes are easily available online.

Office in a wardrobe

you will need

Old double-door wardrobe without drawers and shelves

Sandpaper and paints of your choice (see page 210)

Light furniture wax

Wax brush

Wallpaper

Wallpaper paste

Wallpaper brush

Small cupboard, bedside table or a large crate

MDF board: a standard board measures 120 x 240cm (1.2 x 2.4 yd) so you might need more than 1, depending on how many shelves you install

Pretty shelf supports (I used cast iron, which I spray painted gold)

Screws of varying sizes

Screwdriver

Cordless drill

Gold spray paint (optional)

Lampshade

Hot glue gun

1 Remove the door handles and other fixtures from the inside of the wardrobe, such as rails, hooks and mirrors. Hold onto any that you want to replace later or keep for another project.

2 Prepare and paint the wardrobe, paying particular attention to blemishes and uneven areas. When the paint is dry, apply the wax (see page 210).

3 The inside of the wardrobe would be the perfect place to put a bold-patterned wallpaper. Measure the space carefully and ensure you line up the pattern. Follow the manufacturer's instructions for making and using the wallpaper paste, and hang the wallpaper. .

4 Decide where you would like to have some shelves and a desk top. For this wardrobe, a small cupboard sits inside the wardrobe with a piece of MDF cut to fit resting upon it to make a desk top. Small shelves provide extra storage.

5 Take careful measurements for the length and width of each shelf and either saw the shelves yourself from MDF or ask a professional to do this for you. Measure and position carefully before screwing shelf brackets to the back of the wardrobe to support the shelves. For greater stability, you might choose to screw the shelves to the brackets using the cordless drill.

6 Replace any wardrobe fittings that you want to reuse. For this wardrobe the tie rack and hooks have been spray painted and are now used to hang craft supplies. You could also drill a hole to thread through an extension cable to power a laptop or a desk lamp.

7 For the finishing touches you could stick a lampshade to the top of the wardrobe using a hot glue gun, replace the handles on the outside, hang framed prints or a notice or pinboard (see page 186 and 188).

Creative Spaces

If you work from home, as I do, your creative space or office is somewhere you will find you spend much of your time. Increasingly we are all discovering the joys of working from home, and yet this is often the room that people spend the least time thinking about when it comes to decorating. To many, the study is a room in which there is a desk, a chair, some filing cabinets and perhaps some books, and it can lack soul and personality. But just because the room is dominated by technology and other modern necessities for work, that doesn't mean it can't have a vintage look too.

As I spend the majority of my day in my office, coming up with ideas and designs, as well as doing the less creative admin aspects of running a business, it is important to me that I feel comfortable in the space. Because I love floral wallpaper, that's what I have used to line my walls, and I've tried to make what was a masculine space more feminine by using glass handles on cupboards and painting the wood in a soft green-blue.

If possible, locate your creative space somewhere in the house that has natural light so you don't feel like you're locked away all day. If you have it, a room with a view is lovely – if you know you won't get distracted by what's going on outside! If you do get distracted, cover the window. Lace panels are great as curtains in offices: they look prettier than blinds and are more interesting to look at, while also letting in natural light, softening it as it streams through on sunny days (see page 57).

In a darker room, keep it dark with good lighting. Modern desks can be painted in light or pastel colours to give them a vintage feel, as can cupboards or filing cabinets. If, like me, you find yourself sneaking into your study in the evening when the kids are in bed, think about lighting after dark. A standard or desk lamp is a good idea, but it can be made to look less office-like with a pretty lampshade, or you could be really

decadent and fit the ceiling light with a chandelier. Why not? If it's a room you like spending time in, work then doesn't feel so bad, does it?

Desk and other furniture aside, a comfy chair is essential if you're sitting at the computer all day. You can pick up unusual vintage chairs at auctions, flea markets and on eBay, and if you are inspired by the shape but don't like the covering, or it has seen better days, you could look into having it reupholstered with a fabric that you do like – or even make your own removable cover (see page 117).

A working space has to be kept ordered to minimise distractions, so include some shelving or cupboards to house office essentials. Books look neat lined up on shelves, but knick-knacks, paperwork and stationery can look messy, so try putting them all in baskets or box files covered in your favourite fabrics on the shelves or your desk. Personalise your space with framed pictures or photos of family and friends to make the space less like an office. I have a mood board on the wall in my study on which I've pinned pictures of people who inspire me, swatches of fabrics, bits of lace, wallpaper swatches and paint colour charts. You can do this on a pinboard that you've made yourself, too (see page 187). On a hectic day I find lighting scented candles at my desk is the perfect way to relieve stress, and a jar of freshly picked flowers can bring the outside in when you long to leave the house.

This is a room in which less is most definitely more, but above all it has to be a room that works for the person who works in it. If in doubt, start simple and build up the effect with the furniture and accessories you love until it is a space that really feels like yours. The joy of a home office is that you don't have to think about other people sharing your space and it can be exactly as you want it to be.

feature CREATIVE SPACES

Cork pinboards are perfect for keeping essentials for projects to hand. For example, I use mine for swatches of material or ribbons and to pin notes or measurements. What I particularly like about cork is that it is very lightweight, which makes it easy to hang.

Framed cork pinboard

you will need

Picture frame

Cork board, about the same size as the picture frame and no thicker than the frame

Craft knife

Cutting mat

Hot glue gun

Strong bonding adhesive, picture wire or a D-ring, to hang

1 Remove the glass from the picture frame and dispose of it safely. Remove the stiff board from the back of the picture frame together with any tacks or tape if it is an old frame.

2 Lay the backing board from the frame over the cork board and draw all around it. Using a craft knife and cutting mat, trim the cork to size.

3 Using the hot glue gun, stick the cork board to the frame. If you are hanging the pinboard on the inside of a cupboard door, like I have, then attach it with strong bonding adhesive. If it is to be hung on a wall, fix a picture D-ring or a length of picture wire to the back of the picture frame.

PEARLS *of* WISDOM

I always use pretty pearl-headed pins to make something that can look quite industrial look rather pretty when it is covered with my inspiration and workings.

I'm a very visual person, so a noticeboard for reminders is a great way to make sure I won't forget anything. My noticeboard is like my second diary, but you could also use it as a live mood board or to display photos.

Fabric & ribbon noticeboard

you will need

40 x 30cm (16 x 12in) x 12mm (½in) thick MDF board, cut to size and with the corners removed
4oz density polyester quilting wadding
Staple gun
45 x 35cm (18 x 14in) fabric to cover the front of the board
3–4m (3–4yd) ribbon
Upholstery pins
Hammer
40 x 30cm (16 x 12in) fabric to cover the back of the board
Picture wire or a D-ring, to hang

1 Cut the wadding to the size of the board. Staple it to the MDF, starting at the centre of one narrow edge and moving along the remaining edges of the board.

2 Lay out your fabric, right side down, place the board on top (wadding side down) and then cut the fabric, allowing 2.5–5cm (1–2in) extra all around to wrap it onto the back of the board.

3 Use the staple gun to fix the fabric in place. Work on one edge at a time, always starting in the centre and working out to the edges and keeping the fabric taut. To tidy the corners, pinch the fabric together, fold it down to one edge and staple twice. Trim any excess fabric.

4 To make the ribbon latticework, first cut one length of ribbon to run from corner to corner of the board, on the diagonal, adding 10cm (4in) to the length to wrap onto the back of the board. Staple in place on the back of the board.

5 Repeat with another length of ribbon so that it lies parallel with the first ribbon at a distance of 10cm (4in). Increase or decrease this distance to tailor the size of the gaps in the lattice to what you are choosing to display. Repeat with more lengths of ribbon until you have covered the board in equally-spaced stripes going in one direction.

6 Repeat Steps 4 and 5 for the ribbon strips in the opposite direction.

7 Where two ribbons cross, hammer in an upholstery pin to hold them in place.

8 To cover the back of the board, cut your chosen fabric to the size of the board plus a 2cm (¾in) allowance. Press in 1cm (½in) all the way around and then staple the fabric to the back of the board.

9 Fix a D-ring or a length of picture wire to the back of the board to hang it.

Fabric-covered clips & pins

I read once that beauty can be found in the everyday, so although it may seem a little over the top to upcycle pins and clips, it does make an office space and plain stationery a little more exciting, and is a great way to use up all of those little scraps of fabric or odd buttons.

you will need

Paper clips

Self-covering buttons with shallow shanks, or random odd buttons

Fabric remnants

Felt

Hot glue gun

Miniature or full-size desk pegs

Thick white card

1 For the paper clips, cover the self-covering buttons in fabric remnants following the manufacturer's instructions, or use odd buttons. To back each button, cut out a matching-sized piece of felt and snip two small slits in the centre. Stick the felt to the back of each button using the hot glue gun. Feed the paper clip through the slits in the felt

2 To decorate the pegs, lay out the fabric right side down on your work surface. Cut out small shapes, such as hearts, from the card and stick them onto the fabric with the hot glue gun. Cut around the hearts and attach them to the pegs, again using the glue gun.

If you have rows upon rows of box files or folders on display like I do, it's worth turning them into a feature. This really simple but effective project makes personal admin and filing a little less dull. Use different textures and patterns, and ribbon ties and brass label holders for extra finishing touches.

Fabric-covered box files

you will need

| 2 or 3 A4 box files |
| At least 1sq m (1sq yd) of each fabric design |
| Dressmaker's chalk |
| Double-sided sticky tape |
| Brass label holders (optional) |
| Hot glue gun (optional) |

1 Take the following measurements, referring to the diagram:

> The length of the file lid: measurement A
> The width of the file lid: measurement B
> The depth of the file: measurement C

Then, using these measurements, draw an outline on a single sheet of paper as shown in the diagram, right. Add 5cm- (2in)-wide flaps, where indicated, which will fold inside the box to give a neat finish. Cut around the outline to make a template.

2 Lay out the fabric, right sides up, and place the template on top. Draw around the template with dressmaker's chalk. Remove the template and then cut out the fabric. Attach double-sided sticky tape to the wrong side along the flaps, together with the edges without flaps. Peel off the backing tape and carefully smooth the fabric onto the box. Fold over the flaps and stick them to the inside of the box.

3 If you would like to line the inside of the boxes, repeat Steps 1 and 2, but without the flaps.

4 If you are using brass label holders, stick them on with a hot glue gun.

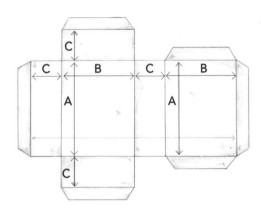

PEARLS *of* WISDOM

I use both paper and fabric for my boxes, but fabric is easier and more hard-wearing, because paper can split at the corners.

Wallpapered mini drawers

Try these ideas with a remnant or two left over from a wallpapering project, or look for vintage patterns at flea markets or in a charity shop. These small drawers are great for storing haberdashery and stationery, and organising small bits and bobs.

you will need

Set of mini drawers

Wallpaper or vintage paper offcuts

Spray glue

1 Take the drawers out of the unit and take off any handles or other fittings that may be attached to them.

2 Measure the height, width and combined length of all sides of the drawer body; draw the outline onto the wallpaper and cut out.

3 Measure the faces of the drawers only, draw the outline onto wallpaper and cut out. Ensure that the placement of any patterns on the wallpaper have been considered before marking and cutting out.

4 Spray glue the pieces of paper, stick them in place and leave to dry for a couple of hours.

5 Replace any handles or labels before using.

Floral Wallpaper

I 've always been into floral wallpaper, but when I first started decorating my homes I was never brave enough to actually put it up for fear of losing the light in a small room.

My love affair with wallpaper (Danny might say obsession, and I think I probably have to agree with him) really began in 2003, when I was staying at a little boutique hotel. I was sleeping in a room that had a beautiful black floral paper on the walls – and I had to ask the owner of the hotel what it was. She very kindly let me buy a few spare rolls from her and when I got back home, I asked my decorator if he could put it up in my bedroom, but he said it would make the room too dark and refused to do it. So the wallpaper sat in a cupboard for a few years until we moved again, where I put it up in my 1950s caravan. It looked spectacular and I immediately got the wallpaper bug.

When we moved into the house we're in now, I decided that this was where I would experiment with wallpaper. The house was a bit too modern for me and I needed to make it look old, so wallpapering everywhere was the perfect solution.

What I've learned about choosing wallpaper over the years is that first and foremost you have to go for what you especially like, then find a place for it. Smaller prints tend to look better in smaller rooms, but big flowers can also look good, so don't get hung up on the scale of the design. There seems to be a modern trend for putting wallpaper up on just one wall to create a feature wall and painting the others, but I think that if you're going to use wallpaper you should use it on every wall. I even wallpaper ceilings, such as for my sons' bedrooms.

There are so many prints available that you can easily find something you like; there are wonderful modern prints that look great with vintage styling, which is something worth bearing in mind. But I still think that vintage prints are the most beautiful – they have real elegance and style. There are well-known companies that sell new rolls of classic vintage prints, including the designs of the great 19th-century designer

William Morris, but if you're willing to do a bit of digging around you can also find vintage rolls online. Websites will sell original rolls, as will sellers on eBay, but be careful when you are ordering that you have measured up correctly and have taken into account the repeat on the pattern if there is one, as once these rolls are gone, they're gone, and it will be very difficult to find them anywhere else. If you fall in love with a design but there aren't enough rolls of it available to cover the whole room, see if you can find another paper that will look good with it and simply paper the room in two different styles.

Using wallpaper seems to have gone out of fashion a bit, but don't be put off; be brave and go for it, and don't worry about convention. If you want to mix stripes with florals or checks, do so – throw it all in together and you'll be amazed what you come out with.

Hold on to beautiful papers from magazines, old cards or wrapping; they are great for embellishing or upcycling tired furniture. Découpage can be really subtle and simple, as with the wooden chair (see page 22), but here the layering of paper cut-outs creates a very different effect.

Découpage magazine holder

(see page 22)

you will need

Lots of patterned paper or pictures for the découpage, such as wrapping paper, wallpaper, magazines, greetings cards, tissue, paper doillies and lace

Item to découpage, such as an old bin or box big enough to fit magazines

Découpage glue

Paintbrush

Tasselled braid, to finish (optional)

Hot glue gun (optional)

1 Select your paper: think about themes and colours and the inside of your holder as well as the outside – a contrasting colour scheme on the inside can be very effective.

2 On a prepared work surface, cut out your découpage motifs. You will need enough for roughly two layers. Paint glue on the back of each motif and stick them to the surface of your magazine holder, using your paintbrush to help position them. Brush over the paper with some extra glue to seal. Build up the layers randomly or following a pattern on both the outside and the inside.

3 When you are happy with the design, leave the magazine holder to dry overnight. Finish by attaching a tasselled braid or other trim all the way around with the hot glue gun. Fill the holder with magazines.

Embossed notelets & envelopes

Creating a set of homemade notelets or cards is a great way to use up scraps of vintage-style papers. To make them even more personal you can emboss a design of your own making on the paper. Leftover wallpaper also works really well for envelopes, as it is nice and thick. A handmade card adds an extra thoughtful touch to any thank-you letter or birthday wish; you could also make a set to give as a gift.

you will need

For the notelets

Stamp (see page 205, or use a ready-made one)

Acrylic stamp pad

Uncoated card, cut to 10 x 15cm (4 x 6in) for each notelet

Embossing powder (I used gold, but there are plenty of other colours to choose from)

Protective gloves

Craft heat gun

For the envelopes

Vintage wallpaper or vintage wrapping paper

Glue or double-sided sticky tape

1 To emboss the notelets, press the stamp into the stamp pad and then press it firmly onto the card to apply the glue. Sprinkle the stamped image liberally with embossing powder and leave for about 10 seconds so that it sticks to the glue. Then carefully tip the excess embossing powder onto the middle of a piece of paper and tip it back into the powder jar. The whole process is just like sticking glitter onto Christmas cards.

2 Wearing the protective gloves, turn on the heat gun and, when it is hot, gently run it over the powdered image. Move it in gentle circles so that the heat doesn't concentrate in one spot, and don't put the gun too near the card. When the embossing powder has changed colour and melted, turn off the gun and set it aside. Always remember to read the manufacturer's guidelines before using the heat gun and ensure the room is well ventilated. Alternatively, you could use ink.

3 Repeat Steps 1 and 2 for as many notelets as you wish to make.

4 To make the envelopes for the notelets, draw two rectangles next to each other measuring 10 x 15cm (4 x 6in) on the back of the envelope paper (these will be the front and back of the envelope).

5 On three sides of one of the rectangles, add a 1.5cm (⅝in) flap. On the opposite rectangle, draw the main flap, which you can make as a straight or diamond-shaped flap.

6 Cut out the paper and fold along all the flaps. Apply glue or double-sided tape to the three flaps to assemble the envelope and leave to dry.

7 Repeat Steps 4 to 6 to make as many envelopes as you have notelets.

8 To keep your writing set in good condition, put your notelets and envelopes into a small box and tie with a ribbon.

I am always writing letters, thank-you messages and little notelets, and a homemade stamp is a fun way to add a personal touch. There are many different materials you can use to make a stamp, from foam to wood and even potatoes – experiment; each one gives a different effect. This stamp is made from rubber lino material.

Personalised rubber stamp

you will need

Piece of rubber lino, large enough for your stamp design
Ballpoint or ink-based pen
Craft knife
Cutting mat
Ink pad

1 Draw your own design on a piece of paper or trace the templates on page 231. It's important to use a ballpoint or ink-based pen.

2 Moisten the rubber lino (it doesn't matter which side of the lino you use) with a sponge dipped in water, and press the lino onto your design or the tracing paper (if you are using the pattern from this book). The ink from the pen will transfer to the lino, which also reverses the design for you. Retrace the design with a ballpoint pen to sharpen the image. (If you are drawing your own design directly onto the lino, remember that it has to be a mirror image. Lettering has to be carefully drawn out in reverse.)

3 Starting with the detailed pieces first and using a cutting mat to protect your work surface, carefully cut into the lino with the craft knife to gently remove the rubber around the design. When cutting a curve or circle you might find it easier to get a smooth line if you keep the blade in one place and move the rubber.

4 When you have finished, gently brush off the loose bits of rubber and blow on the stamp to remove any remaining fine pieces.

5 To test the stamp, put the rubber on the ink pad, making sure to apply a full and even coat of ink, and press the stamp firmly onto some scrap paper (you may need to repeat this step to achieve a complete impression the first time round). Carve away more of the rubber if necessary, to finish.

PEARLS *of* WISDOM

To make the stamp easier to use, stick a wooden block or offcut to the back of your stamp with a hot glue gun to make a handle. You can even decorate it if you like.

Craft Basics

Basic craft kit

Having a well-stocked craft kit at the ready is essential. Once you have the basics you can introduce more unusual supplies and materials to your collection. Keep hold of offcuts of fabric, sample pots of paint and broken jewellery. With the right tools in your craft kit and a little inspiration, you can craft and upcycle almost anything. These must-have basics are easily available from good art and craft shops and online.

Beads, buttons and bows Perfect for adding detail and embellishment to your craft makes.

Craft knife and cutting mat Wonderful for fiddly jobs, when you need a little more precision than scissors can offer. Make sure you keep some spare blades in store, too. A cutting mat with a measuring grid is also extremely useful and protects the table underneath. Craft knife blades are extremely sharp, so be careful!

D-cut squeegee These useful wooden handles with rubber edging are perfect for textile printing, as the shape of the blade ensures a heavier deposit of ink.

Découpage glue Useful for découpage, scrapbooking and paper crafting. Can also be used as a sealant and a varnish.

Disposable cleaning cloths Wet cleaning cloths and bits of old rag are perfect for cleaning or dusting down your vintage finds. It is also important to keep surfaces clean and tidy while you work.

Embroidery hoops These come in different sizes, but an average-sized 15cm (6in) hoop is the most useful.

Hot glue gun and glue sticks Possibly one of the most useful bits of kit you can invest in, a hot glue gun is especially useful for the bigger interiors projects. Make sure you stock up on glue sticks. Always remember to read the manufacturer's guidelines and wear protective clothing – the glue can get very hot.

Masking tape Easy to tear yet durable, masking tape is essential for keeping stencils in place, marking off edges to ensure a clean finish when painting wooden furniture and securing backing.

Paints It is always useful to have a basic range of paints to hand. At the very least, keep a small can of primer, undercoat and your preferred finish for a top coat (see page 210) in your craft kit. Keep an eye open for reduced tester pots at DIY stores; they can be very useful indeed.

Paintbrushes, in all sizes Build a good selection of paintbrushes, ranging from small brushes useful for painting delicate designs to large brushes suitable for painting wooden furniture. I also recommend that you buy the best brushes you can afford, and look after them. Make sure you clean them thoroughly each time you use them and store them somewhere flat. For information about preparing and painting wooden surfaces, see page 210.

Sewing kit See below.

Sewing machine Although most of the projects in this book can be hand sewn, there are times when using a machine may be quicker or give you a better finish. You can buy a new machine or pick up a really good secondhand one relatively affordably. Alternatively, you can pay to use a sewing machine by the hour at some sewing cafés and craft shops.

Staple gun Absolutely essential for furniture projects and handy for woodwork projects. Be careful when using and always read the manufacturer's instructions.

Sticky tape Single and double-sided tape is essential.

Stippling brush (for stencilling) This is a brilliant specialist brush with short, firmly-packed bristles. Available in a variety of widths, they are the only brushes to use when stencilling because the short, stiff bristles reduce the chance of getting paint under the edge of the stencil.

Tracing paper For transferring images and templates onto paper and fabrics.

Vintage braids, ribbons and trims I keep metres of old braids on cotton spools – they add the perfect finish to so many small craft and furniture projects and also hide a multitude of sins.

Water-soluble markers For making marks on fabrics, glassware, tiles and china that can then be washed off.

Wax and wax brush If you enjoy upcycling furniture, it is worth keeping a tin of wax (in fact, two tins: one light and one dark, depending on what you are waxing) and a wax brush to hand. Wax gives the perfect vintage finish to any piece of painted wood. It also offers a protective layer.

Essential sewing kit

I have all manner of things in my sewing kit. However, these are the essentials you will need, especially if you are new to sewing.

Dressmaker's chalk A really great way of clearly marking fabric. I recommend having a dark and a light piece of chalk for different colours of fabric. The chalk can be brushed or washed off.

Needles There are many different types of needle, ranging from large blunt tapestry needles to medium-length sharps. I recommend buying a mixed packet from your local haberdashery store to get you started.

Pins Safety pins and straight sewing pins – and plenty of them. You will always need more than you think, particularly when working on larger pieces of fabric. I like to use slightly decorative pins even for simple tasks like hemming as they are easy to spot against a patterned fabric background. Keep in a special tin.

Scissors Small embroidery, general-purpose (ideally a medium size) and dressmaking scissors (ideally large) are invaluable. Keep for sewing only, to avoid blunting the blade too quickly.

Tape measure A non-stretchy canvas one is the best, but for smaller pieces you could use a ruler.

Thimble Perfect for protecting your index finger or thumb when working on sewing projects.

Threads When it comes to choosing a colour for a sewing project, a good tip is to use a shade slightly darker than the fabric when it is a strong colour, and a shade slightly lighter than the fabric for paler patterns.

Basic sewing stitches

Securing thread by overstitching

1 To start (and finish) a row of stitches, sew the thread through the fabric, leaving a few millimetres free at the end (you can trim this off later).

2 Stitch over the stitch you have just made a few times. The stitches you have just created will fasten the loose end.

Running Stitch

This is the most basic stitch. It can be used to hem fabric, sew seams, as a decorative embroidery stitch or to gather fabric.

1 Secure the thread and bring the needle through to the right side where you wish your line of stitches to begin.

2 Push the needle back through to the reverse a short distance away. The distance will determine how long your stitch is.

3 Bring the needle back to the right side a short distance from the first stitch. The distance from the end of the first stitch will determine the space between your stitches.

4 Repeat Steps 2 and 3 until you have sewn your row. While it is usual to keep each of the stitches the same size, you can change this for different effects by varying the lengths of the stitches or the gaps as you progress along the row.

Slip Stitch

This stitch is very versatile, as it can be used for hemming, appliqué and general mending. The purpose is to stitch one fold of fabric to another nearly invisibly, creating a blind stitch.

1 Secure the thread and slip the needle into the folded fabric, bringing it up through the fabric on the top fold.

2 Put the needle into the folded fabric, gather about four to five of the fabric threads and then bring the thread back through towards the hem edge.

3 Next, point the needle back into the folded fabric, close to where you drew the needle out, evenly picking up the threads of the fabric in the same direction on each stitch.

4 Put the needle into the folded fabric, gather

about four to five of the fabric threads and then bring the thread back through.

5 Repeat Steps 2 to 4 until you have sewn your row.

Blanket Stitch

This is a classic edging stitch for blankets and quilts, but it can also be used to hem two pieces of fabric together, and gives a pretty effect when sewn large and in colourful, contrasting thread.

1 Secure the thread and bring the needle through to the right side where you wish your line of stitches to begin.

2 Push the needle through to the wrong side where you wish the loop of your first blanket stitch to finish.

3 Pull the needle through, but before you pull the thread through behind it, thread the needle back towards the front side through the loop. Pull the thread through to form your first blanket stitch.

4 Repeat Steps 2 and 3 along the seam or edge. To finish your row of blanket stitches, complete your last stitch then bring the needle over to the wrong side of the fabric and either secure it neatly (if sewing along an edge) or push the needle back through the last stitch and thread through between the layers of fabric and secure (if sewing a seam).

Back Stitch

Back stitch forms a continuous line of small end-to-end stitches. It can either be used as a decorative stitch or to hand sew a seam where something a little stronger than running stitch is required.

1 Secure the thread and bring the needle through to the right side where you wish your line of stitches to begin.

2 Return the needle through to the wrong side a short distance away. The distance will determine how long your stitch is.

3 Bring the needle back to the right side, leaving a gap the same size as your initial stitch.

4 Return the needle to the wrong side at the end of the initial stitch, effectively going back on yourself, so you have two stitches of equal length running end to end. There should be no gap between the stitches.

5 Repeat Steps 2 to 4 until you have sewn your row. While it is usual to sew each of the stitches the same size, you can change this to create different effects by varying the lengths as you progress along the row.

Cross-Stitch

Cross-stitch is a form of embroidery where X-shaped stitches are formed in a tiled pattern to make a picture or design. Fabrics used for cross-stitch include aida and linen, and mixed-content fabrics called 'evenweave'. These fabrics are categorised by threads per inch (referred to as the 'count'), which can range from 11- to 40-count. You can also buy soluble canvas that makes working cross-stitch on a fabric such as linen considerably more straightforward.

You can work cross-stitches from left to right or from right to left, but always ensure that the lower half of each cross lies in one direction, starting from the same side for each stitch, or else you will get an uneven finish.

1 Secure the thread.

2 Working on the canvas holes in groups of four, bring the needle up through one of the bottom holes and take it down through the canvas in the hole diagonally opposite (a).

3 Bring the needle back to the front again one hole down. You now have a half-cross.

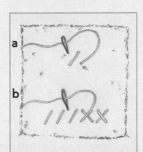

4 Repeat Steps 2 and 3 along the row of stitches on the chart, and then work your way back to complete the upper section of the crosses (b).

Preparing and painting wood

When restoring or repainting any wooden object, whether it be a small crate or a larger piece of furniture such as chest of drawers or a wardrobe, it is always very important to prepare the wood. Here is a step-by-step guide to getting the perfect finish.

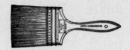

Cover up For many of the projects, especially when there is paint involved, you will need to protect your work surface thoroughly with sheets of newspaper or an old sheet. You might want to wear overalls, too – it's remarkable just how far paint and other splashy liquids travel.

Preparation Start by sanding the wood, first with coarse sandpaper and then moving through medium and fine grades until you achieve a beautifully smooth finish. Wipe over the surfaces with a damp cloth to remove all dust and leave to dry.

Painting For any new wood with knots in, apply some knot sealant before anything else. Leave it to dry. If you are painting onto bare wood, and are looking for the best finish, it is best to apply a coat of primer. Bare wood is very absorbent and this helps further coats of paint go on more smoothly. However, for a more vintage, aged feel, you may want to skip the primer.

Follow with a layer of undercoat (light or dark, depending on the colour you are painting over it) and for the top coat, you can choose between satin- or matt-finish gloss and chalk-based paints. I like to use the latter for a great vintage-style finish. Always let each coat of paint dry thoroughly before applying another coat.

Waxing As most of the paints I use are chalk based, I like to finish them with water-repellent wax in either a light or dark finish, depending on the colour of the paint and the effect I want to create. You can also buy wax brushes, which make applying the wax much easier. After you have waxed the surface, use a lint-free cloth to work the wax into the surface and buff.

Sourcing & Salvaging Vintage

Over the years I have found vintage stuff everywhere. I've made some mistakes (which I've always learned from) and I've also bought some absolute bargains, so here are a few tips for buying vintage or vintage-style.

Get ready to start shopping!

The most important thing about buying vintage is to do your research before you buy anything big or expensive, but also to keep a lookout everywhere you go – whether it's on a shopping trip, a day out or even on holiday.

Genuine vintage goods are, by their nature, often unique and so you will find that sometimes you see something and you have to buy it there and then or lose it for ever. That's fine, as long as you accept that you might find yourself overpaying if you aren't savvy. The joy of modern technology is that often you can google something to check a price before you commit to buying, but if it's something cheap and cheerful, you may be happy to bypass that.

However, if you are looking to buy something more expensive, something that is perhaps more of a statement piece, it pays to do your research first. Take a look around to see what sort of prices are being paid for similar pieces before you agree a price with a seller. The internet is a wonderful tool for this, and in particular eBay, which allows you to get a good overview of what people are charging and for what condition.

Where to buy

There are loads of different places to buy from – ranging from the smart (and thus sometimes pricey) to the cheap and cheerful.

At the top end of the scale are antique dealers. If you are going for antiques from a smart shop, be aware that some outlets will charge a premium if they are in expensive areas, such as central London, so you won't necessarily be getting a bargain. That said, you may find something unique, which makes it worth the overspend, and you might also be able to strike a deal – it's always worth asking the dealer what is their best price, and they may even be open to negotiation (see page 215 for tips on haggling!).

Antique auction houses and local antique dealers often are cheaper than those in cities, but be warned that this isn't always the case and you can find prices get hiked up if there is a bidding war for something. They are worth a look, though, even if it is only to get an idea of what sort of prices pieces are going for. When you buy from any shop or auction house, always get a receipt for your goods, ensuring that it lists the age of the piece you are buying, the price you paid, and any damage you can see on it that might affect its value.

Antique shops often stock the crème de la crème of vintage gear, but I've found a lot of other sources for my original pieces over the years, which are a lot cheaper, and often the quality is just as good.

My favourite places to buy are at flea markets and vintage fairs. I can spend hours wandering round stalls and picking my way through all their lovely treasures. There are always lots of these sales going on regularly throughout the year, and your best bet is to google your local area to find out when the next one is on that is nearest to you. Have a really good rummage around at these events and you might find some hidden gems. As well as lots of wonderful vintage goodies, sellers also often have baskets of offcuts of lace or other textiles, doorknobs and sometimes damaged or mismatched china. Don't ignore these – this is where the bargains are to be had, and if they aren't quite perfect or don't quite go with each other, don't discard them; just think imaginatively about how you could use them. For example, it's quite hard to find vintage tiles with the same pattern in sufficient quantities to cover a specific area, but you can mix and match them or space them out between plain-coloured tiles. If you are artistic, or the pattern is quite simple, you might even be able to copy it on a few tiles to complete the effect.

Charity shops and car boot sales can also be little treasure troves, and here you really do have the opportunity to get a great deal, because many sellers may just see the stuff they are selling as junk, and they may not know the real value of what they are selling. If you're looking for pretty china, this is where you can fill your crockery cupboard inexpensively. Go armed with cash and get ready to haggle!

Buying online

In recent years I've probably had most success on eBay, but there are many other online places you can buy from. You do run the risk here of receiving something that isn't what you were expecting, so if you do have the opportunity to look at something before you part with your cash, then do so. It can be very expensive to return something once it has been delivered, or to have to get rid of it if it really isn't what you want. If you can't see it before you buy, make sure there is a returns policy in place that won't cost you a fortune. If you buy something from abroad, remember to allow for any shipping and duty or tax costs that might be added by the seller or by UK customs, as this can significantly increase the cost of the item.

Salvaging

If you're looking for garden ware or bathroom furniture and accessories, salvage yards can be a great resource. They are also brilliant for old bits of wood, tiles, doors, fireplaces, chairs and sometimes tables. Again, it's a bit of luck as to what is there on the day, but if you are looking for something specific, it's worth striking up a relationship with the owner and seeing if they can give you a call when the things you want come in.

If you know there is building work going on in your local area, keep an eye out for what goes into the skip. Many builders will be delighted to see bulky objects disappearing out of the skip and sparing them the disposal costs, but always ask first to make sure they aren't intending to sell it themselves or use it elsewhere. Private homes being modernised can be great sources of period pieces, such as fireplaces and tiles, but keep an eye out too for any demolition or refitting of old churches and schools, which can yield wonderful old stones, chairs, pews and bits of wood and flooring.

Be brave – if you don't ask you don't get, so don't feel embarrassed; the worst they can say is no. Recently we were having lunch at Babington House in Somerset and noticed they were removing the old decking boards from around the swimming pool. A few words were exchanged and now those boards have been spliced and hammered into our new steps from the kitchen into the garden!

Before you do the deal

Before you buy anything, always ask the seller if it needs any work doing to it – beyond any obvious damage you can see. If you are buying a piece that needs work, think about how much must be done before you buy. Ideally, you should get a quote for the work from a specialist (if it's something you can't do yourself) before you agree a price. You can find that you buy something inexpensively but then pay more than it cost just to get it how you want it. That's OK if it is still under the market value, but it's annoying if costs then spiral.

If you are buying anything electric, like lights, do make sure that they work with modern systems. There's nothing worse than getting home with a gorgeous lamp or chandelier, only for an electrician to shake his head and tell you it won't work. Be cautious, too, about taps and other fixtures and fittings – make sure they will work with the sink or bath you have in mind. Plumbing and electrical work can come up as some of the most expensive labour costs.

Tips for getting the best deal

Know your stuff before you open the negotiations. Be confident that you know what you are buying, what it is worth and how much you are willing to pay for it.

Really study a piece before you buy it to make sure it is exactly as you would expect it to be. If you don't mind a bit of damage, that's fine, but if you do like things to look in good shape, inspect it carefully so you don't find any flaws later. Pick it up, handle it and look it over. If there is any damage, you can use this to negotiate a lower price.

Begin by asking the seller for their best price on the item.

Try to cultivate a poker face! If you've fallen in love with something, don't let it show. Try to look uncommitted and you will find the seller will be more inclined to lower the price. If they sense how much you want it, they will know you will go higher on the price than you're letting on. Hesitating and looking unconvinced are your best weapons.

Don't start with your best price. Start lower, at about half your maximum, as this gives you more room for negotiation.

Give as little as possible, but know when you are about to reach deadlock. If you can see the seller is not shifting any more and is starting to get irritated by the negotiations, it's probably time to do the deal. Don't be greedy unless you really don't mind whether you get the piece or not. If you really think the final offer is too high, see if you can get the seller to throw something else into the deal.

In all negotiations, be polite – you might want to buy from the seller again and so it's better to create a good relationship with them, which may lead to better deals later, than to push the dealer for a deal now and be blackballed by them.

Ultimately, the key thing to remember when buying vintage is to buy it because you love it, not because it is fashionable or might make you some money one day. If something makes you smile when you see it, it won't disappoint you if you try to sell it and don't make a profit. Personally, I don't like having things in my house that I don't really like – they just take up space where I could put something else that I really want.

Pearl's
LITTLE BLACK BOOK
of shops & suppliers

Vintage originals & antiques

Alfie's Antiques Market
alfiesantiques.com; 020 7723 6066
Huge indoor market in London, NW8, where more than 75 dealers sell a wide range of antiques and collectables.

Anne Fowler Antiques
annefowlertetbury.co.uk; 01666 504043
Amazing antique shop in Tetbury, Gloucestershire, which sells fabulous home accessories and pieces for the house and garden.

Antiques & Country Living
43–44 Vallis Way, Frome, BA11 3BA; 01373 463015
A mixture of old and new; fantastic for home accessories, unusual gifts and antique china.

Baileys
baileyshomeandgarden.com; 01989 561931
Visit the online shop or their old farm buildings in Herefordshire for vintage and recycled homewares and accessories.

B & T Antiques
bntantiques.co.uk; 020 7229 7001
Antique dealer in London's Notting Hill which has a fabulous collection of French mirrors and Art Deco mirrored furniture.

Betty and Violet
bettyandviolet.com
Gorgeous vintage textiles, pillows and accessories.

Camden markets
camdenmarkets.org
Alternative fashion, vintage and new designers for furniture and clothing.

Chloe Antiques and Interiors
chloeantiques.co.uk; 01985 213077

Fabulous French and Swedish painted furniture, accessories and textiles.

Cloth House
clothhouse.com; 020 7437 5155
A treasure trove in central London of vintage textiles and fabrics from around the world. Plus buttons, ribbons and trimmings for crafty projects.

Cobbled Yard Vintage Store
cobbled-yard.co.uk; 020 8809 5286
It's well worth a visit to this stable-block in Stoke Newington, which is packed with vintage and retro furniture as well as accessories.

Crowman Antiques
crowmandevizes.co.uk; 01380 725548
Shop in Devizes selling lots of old books, lights, rugs, china and stuffed animals.

Dairy House Antiques
www.dairyhouseantiques.co.uk; 01747 853317
Over 25 dealers of antique furniture, lighting, rugs, books, china, jewellery and other collectables.

Daisy Roots Vintage
daisyrootsvintage.co.uk; 01409 211465
Vintage linens, china, glass and enamelware.

Darby & Joan
darbyandjoanvintage.co.uk; 07976 409518
Beautiful candles, vintage china and accessories for sale or hire.

Decorative Country Living
decorativecountryliving.com; 01400 273632
Vintage and vintage-style furniture, eiderdowns, enamelware and accessories.

Dotty Moos Country Home Emporium
dottymoos.co.uk; 01380 727666
Wiltshire-based shop selling original vintage and antique furniture and interior accessories.

Eversley Barn Antiques
eversleybarnantiques.co.uk; 0118 932 8518
Hampshire-based antiques barn selling furniture, china,
linen, mirrors etc.

Garden House Antiques
Saddler's Row, Petworth GU28 0AN; 01798 345175
Lots of quilts and antique finds. Carla, the owner of this
Petworth shop, has the best eye.

Gingerlily
gingerlily.co.uk; 0843 216 9902
Wonderful silk duvets, quilts and bed linen.

Haus
haus-interiors.co.uk; 01428 653336
A lovely vintage interiors shop in Haslemere, Hampshire.

Hesta Nesta
hestanesta.co.uk
Vintage textiles, mannequins and clothing – perfect for
dressing-up rooms.

Holt Harrison
holtharrison.co.uk; 01373 474520
Ranch-style products, cow hides, blankets and
feathered hangings in a fabulous shop in Bath.

Homes and Dreams
homesanddreams.co.uk; 01977 613256
Vintage and vintage-style home accessories and
homewares.

Howie and Belle
howieandbelle.com; 020 8964 4553
Antique furniture, mirrors and lighting. Visits
to the London shop are by appointment only, so
call first.

Judith Michael & Daughter Vintage Treasures
judithmichael.com; 020 7722 9000
Brimming with antique and vintage treasures; the
perfect destination for unique items.

Kilver Court
kilvercourt.com; 01749 340422
Designer emporium in Shepton Mallet, which also
stocks vintage furniture, including old desks, tables,
chairs and old pictures.

Kiss the Frog Again
kissthefrogagain.co.uk; 01225 315157
An eclectic shop in Bath full of lovely vintage finds,
desks, throws, cabinets and bags.

La Belle Etoffe
labelleetoffe.co.uk; 01373 453303
Fabulous showroom in Frome stuffed with
French armoires, cabinets and 1930s leather
club chairs.

La Belle Maison
jeffinie-labellemaison.blogspot.co.uk; 07903 173045
Wonderful north-Dorset shop selling bespoke
handpainted and shabby chic furniture and vintage and
French collectables.

Les Couilles du Chien
lescouillesduchien.com; 020 8968 0099
An eclectic mix of antique furniture and accessories
available to buy or hire.

Llewelyn & Co
llewelynandcompany.com; 01497 821880
Antique French furniture, mirrors and decorative
vintage home and garden ware for sale from their
Hay-on-Wye shop.

Make & Mend
stcatherinesfrome.co.uk/shops; 07966 073213
A real mix of vintage clothes and furniture.

Mrs Stokes Vintage China
mrsstokes.com; 07769 707636
Vintage china for sale and also for hire for tea parties
and other events.

Odd Limited
www.oddlimited.com; 01993 830 674
Lots of wonderful tribal rugs, tents and garden furniture,
including the fabulous Old Rocker swing seat.

Oh So Vintage
ohsovintage.co.uk; 02392 347818
Authentic vintage and antiques, specialising in French
kitchenalia, eiderdowns and linens.

Ollie's
69 Golborne Road, London, W10; 07768 790725
The most eclectic array of vintage mirrors, chests
and wardrobes.

Original House
original-house.co.uk; 01451 860281
Specialists in reclaimed furniture, lighting and
accessories as well as antique painted French furniture.

Phillips & Skinner
19 High St, Bruton, Somerset, BA10 0AH; 01749 813221
An array of china, glasses, furniture and vintage clothes,
with lots of South American goodies mixed in; I highly
recommend a visit to this shop.

Pimpernel & Partners
pimpernelandpartners.co.uk; 020 7731 2448
French armchairs, sofas, garden furniture, mirrors and
painted shelves and cupboards.

Poppy Greens
poppygreens.co.uk; 01458 860500
Vintage lights, old stamps, glassware and tables and
chairs to hire; baking and flower-arranging courses.

Poot
www.stcatherinesfrome.co.uk/shops; 07905 899514
High-quality vintage clothing and accessories from the 1930s to the 1980s.

RE
re-foundobjects.com; 01434 634567
Vintage homeware, textiles, lighting and accessories.

Retrouvius
retrouvius.com; 020 8960 6060
Architectural salvage that has been reconditioned or reused. A constantly changing stock.

Rockett St George
rockettstgeorge.co.uk; 01444 253391
Brilliant for vintage and vintage-inspired retro lighting and accessories.

Ruby Lane
rubylane.com
US site selling vintage accessories and antiques.

Samaya Ling Vintage
samayalingvintage.com; 011798 55551
Stunning rare and unique vintage clothing and accessories.

Sera Hersham-Loftus
seraoflondon.com; 07977 534115
Interior designer with a romantic, seductive style.

Summerill & Bishop
summerillandbishop.com; 020 7229 1337
Vintage linens, glass- and enamelware sourced from French markets.

Susannah Decorative Antiques and Textiles
cloudsandangels.com; 01225 445069
Susannah's shop in Bath is full of French antique finds and lots of lace, as well as her own creations such as hearts, cushions and baskets made from vintage fabrics.

The Antique Shop
5 High Street, Bruton, Somerset, BA10 0AB; 01749 813264
Great for vintage jewellery and lights – lots of gorgeous chandeliers.

The Cross
thecrossshop.co.uk; 020 7727 6760
Lifestyle boutique in west London with an eclectic mix of fashion, accessories for the home and kidswear.

The Dining Room Shop
thediningroomshop.co.uk; 020 8878 1020
Everything for the vintage table: china, glass, silver, linens, lights and candles.

The Last Place on Earth
37 Bramley Road, London, W10; 07958 244609
A fantastic shop, full of reworked furniture. Everything is restored, handpainted and distressed.

The Oxford Tea Party
theoxfordteaparty.com; 0800 292 2734
Everything you need for a vintage tea party, from teacups to teapots. Also sells books and jewellery.

The Shabby Barn
theshabbybarn.co.uk; 01953 681075
Shabby chic furniture, painted vintage furniture and homewares.

The Vintage Pavilion
thevintagepavilion.com; 01344 861942
A Berkshire bar full of traders of vintage and vintage-style accessories, collectables and handmade crafts.

Through the Cottage Door
throughthecottagedoor.co.uk; 07944 351852
Shabby chic furniture and homewares and original accessories.

Vi Spring Mattresses
vispring.co.uk; 01752 366311
The comfiest mattresses in the world.

Wells Trading Post
wellstradingpost.com; 01749 671454
Four floors of the best vintage finds, from clothes to stuffed animals. A real treasure trove in Wells, Somerset.

Vintage & vintage-style

Anthropologie
www.anthropologie.eu
Vintage-style homewares, clothes, jewellery and accessories.

Berry Red
berryred.co.uk; 0845 450 3937
Vintage-inspired and vintage original home accessories, including quilts, cushions and throws.

Beyond France
beyondfrance.co.uk; 01285 641867
Vintage fabrics and table linens from around the world.

Cabbages & Roses
cabbagesandroses.com; 020 7352 2444
Modern and vintage linens, cushions and accessories.

Cath Kidston
cathkidston.co.uk; 0845 026 2440
Classic vintage-style gifts, fabrics and homewares.

Cox & Cox
coxandcox.co.uk; 0844 858 0744

Decorative furniture and accessories inspired by childhood memories.

eBay
ebay.co.uk
Online marketplace to buy and sell almost anything.

Etsy
etsy.com
Online international marketplace for handmade and original crafts, supplies and vintage items.

Emily Rose Vintage
emilyrosevintage.co.uk
Upcycled bespoke furniture and homewares.

Froufrou & Thomas
froufrouandthomas.co.uk; 01935 825124
Beautiful traditional designers of Christmas crackers.

Graham & Green
grahamandgreen.co.uk; 0845 130 6622
Globally-inspired furniture and home accessories with a 1930s feel.

Ikea
ikea.com
Well-priced modern furniture and accessories, perfect for upcycling.

Jessica Lennox
jessicalennox.co.uk
Bone china homewares and textiles designed with countryside illustrations.

Laura Ashley
lauraashley.com; 0871 983 5999
Traditional and vintage-inspired homewares and furnishings.

Lauren Moriarty
laurenmoriarty.co.uk; 0207 5311431
Beautiful, original accessories for the home.

Lou Rota
lourota.com
Upcycled vintage china and vintage-style designs for tableware.

Magnolia Pearl
magnoliapearl.com
Vintage-style clothes and accessories, online but based in America.

Martha Stewart
marthastewart.com
Inspirational ideas for creative arts and crafts for the home.

Nostalgia at the Stone House
nostalgiaatthestonehouse.blogspot.co.uk

Handcrafted accessories and furniture made from vintage pieces.

Not on the High Street
notonthehighstreet.com; 0845 2591359
An online marketplace for over 3,000 traders selling vintage and handmade accessories.

Pedlars
pedlars.co.uk; 01330 850400
Gorgeous new vintage-style accessories for the home and garden.

Pinterest
pinterest.com
An inspirational mood board website where people share their 'pinboards' of pictures, looks and styles that inspire them. Follow me at pinterest.com/pearllowedesign/

Rachel Ashwell
rachelashwellshabbychiccouture.com; 0800 516 4309
Bedding, home furnishings and vintage accessories, including vintage restoration work.

Rustic Angels
rusticangels.co.uk; 020 8239 1134
Vintage-style, shabby chic and retro accessories for the home.

Sharp and Noble
sharpandnoble.co.uk; 01980 621145
Vintage and bespoke upholstered furniture made using gorgeous fabrics.

Spotted Sparrow
spottedsparrow.com; 0191 645 1090
Vintage-style stationery, cards and affordable art.

The French House
thefrenchhouse.net; 020 7831 1111
Beautiful rustic and vintage-style homewares crafted by French artisans and their families.

Vicky Trainor
vickytrainor.co.uk; 01642 491087
Vintage-inspired stationery using re-loved, recycled, re-stitched and reinvented haberdashery and linen.

Welbeck Tiles
welbeck.com; 01736 762000
A highly unique, eclectic collection of vintage-style tiles.

Zoë Darlington
zoedarlington.co.uk; 07739 015346
Beautiful handmade lamps inspired by old heirlooms but updated for a more modern taste.

Wallpaper, textiles, paint & paper

Anna French
annafrench.co.uk; 0800 223 0704
Designer of wallpapers, fabrics and lace.

Annie Sloan
anniesloan.com; 01865 202 494
Unique range of chalk paints in a wide range of colours.

Carey Lind
careylinddesign.com
Traditional-style wallpaper with a modern twist.

Celia Birtwell
celiabirtwell.com; 020 7221 0877
Retro-style fabrics and wallpapers.

Cole and Son
cole-and-son.com; 020 7376 4628
Classic and contemporary wallpaper designs.

Elanbach
elanbach.com; 0161 833 3271
New collections every season of vintage-inspired wallpapers and textiles, but no line is ever discontinued.

Farrow and Ball
farrow-ball.com; 01202 876141
Handcrafted paint and wallpaper in traditional designs and colour. Suppliers to the National Trust with a line in their name.

Faye Chadburn
fayesuzannah.co.uk
Mural artist based in Brighton who painted the gypsy-style designs on my caravan.

GF Smith
gfsmith.com; 020 7394 4660
Coloured and textured papers for design or printing.

House of Hackney
houseofhackney.com; 020 7241 0928
Luxury vintage-style wallpaper, bed linen and homewares.

James Hare
james-hare.com; 01132 431 204
Beautiful lace, silk and other fabrics.

John Lewis
johnlewis.com; 08456 049 049
A huge range of vintage-style homewares and fabrics.

Kate Forman
kateforman.co.uk; 01962 732244
French-influenced furniture, faded linens and wallpapers and vintage-style accessories.

Lewis & Wood
lewisandwood.co.uk; 01453 878517
Gloucester-based company designing original vintage-style wallpapers and fabrics.

Linenworks
thelinenworks.com; 020 7819 7620
Gorgeous linens for every room in the house at reasonable prices. Lots of lovely pastel colours.

Little Greene
littlegreene.com; 0845 880 5855
Luxury paints and wallpapers, including their English Heritage line.

Miss Print
missprint.co.uk; 01277 350581
Retro-style wallpapers and fabrics.

Oh Sew Helena
ohsewhelena.co.uk
Sewing services and soft furnishings.

Osborne & Little
osborneandlittle.com
Traditional-style and pretty floral fabrics, wallpapers and home accessories from a range of designers.

Parna
parna.co.uk; 01865 522272
Products including table linens, napkins and cushions, made by artisans using vintage and antique textiles from around the world.

Ralph Lauren
ralphlaurenhome.com
Luxurious paints, wallpapers and fabrics. Well worth the money every now and then!

Rosie's Vintage Wallpaper
rosiesvintagewallpaper.com
Authentic vintage wallpaper dating from the 1900s to the 1970s.

Sandersons
sanderson-uk.com
Classic designs including collections by William Morris, taken from his original designs or inspired by them.

Select Wallpaper
selectwallpaper.co.uk; 01382 477 000
A one-stop shop for wallpaper – over 25,000 patterns available through the website from a wide range of designers.

Sew White
sewwhite.com; 07772 286043
Gorgeous crafts and accessories.

Supernice
supernice.co.uk; 020 7613 3890
Brilliant for wall graphics and wallpaper silhouettes.

Vintage Linens
vintage-linens.co.uk; 01947 601556
Authentic linens and lace as well as accessories and collectables for the home.

Wallpaper Direct
wallpaperdirect.co.uk
Another great one-stop shop for wallpapers by a wide
range of designers at good prices.
What Delilah Did
whatdelilahdid.bigcartel.com
Stylish vintage cross-stitch patterns and kits.
Zoffany
zoffany.com; 0844 543 4748
Elegant and historic designs for paints, wallpapers
and fabrics.

Vintage hire, cakes & flowers

Bramble & Wild
brambleandwild.com; 01373 473788
Vintage and rustic florist based in Frome, Somerset.
Doily Days
doilydays.co.uk; 07795 076553
Vintage china hire, from teacups to teapots and full
country-garden dressing for events.
Elsie Florence
elsieflorence.co.uk; 01963 32752
Vintage crockery hire and styling.
Everything Stops for Tea
everythingstopsfortea.com; 01629 821822
Sellers of antique and vintage tableware from 1780
to 1960.
Foxy Brown's Cakes and Bakes
foxybrown.co.uk
Wonderful layer cakes and cupcakes
Primrose Bakery
primrosebakery.org.uk; 020 7483 4222
Gorgeous and delicious cakes and cupcakes.
Scarlet and Violet
www.scarletandviolet.com
Florists for homes and events.
Susie Bell
beyondbeleaf.co.uk
Beautiful, believable faux flowers.
The Blossom Tree
theblossomtree.co.uk; 01332 864200
Beautiful and original flowers, inspired by the
British countryside.
The Real Flower Company
realflowers.co.uk; 01730 818300
Hampshire-based, vintage- and rustic-style florist.
Vintage Marquees
vintagemarquees.co.uk; 07921 810396

Hire of traditional wooden-pole marquees and shabby
chic accessories.

Flea markets & reclamation

For fairs and flea markets, look on the internet or in local
newspapers for local events and venues. Contact the fair
or organiser or check the website close to the date to
make sure the event is going ahead at the stated venue.

There are also some general websites you can try:
antiqueweb.co.uk
antiques-atlas.com
discovervintage.co.uk; 0113 345 8699
iacf.co.uk (International Antique and Collector's Fairs);
01636 702326
judysvintagefair.co.uk
thevintagedirectory.co.uk; 0121 243 4912
thevintageguidetobritain.wordpress.com
ukvintagefairs.com; 020 8404 0711
vintagefairsuk.co.uk

Salvage

Antique Bathrooms of Ivybridge
antiquebaths.com; 01752 698250
Restored and reproduction baths and bathroom
accessories online and in Devon.
Frome Reclamation
fromerec.co.uk; 01373 463919
Incredible Victorian fireplaces, roll-top baths, doors,
flooring – the lot! Really reasonably priced, as well.
Glastonbury Reclamation
glastonburyreclamation.co.uk; 01458 831122
Specialising in the supply of quality reclaimed building
materials, architectural salvage and country furniture.
UKAA Ltd
ukarchitecturalantiques.com; 01543 222 923
The UK's largest online stock of architectural antiques,
garden antiques, reclamation and salvage.
Wells Reclamation
wellsreclamation.com; 01749 677087
Another great place in Somerset to find baths, kitchens,
sinks – you name it.

Templates & Patterns

As well as all the templates and patterns you will need you will also find a collection of extra motifs that you can use as stencils, embroidery outlines, découpage paper, or use in any way you want to to enhance and add detail to your projects. Use a photocopier or trace freehand to enlarge as required.

Glass-painted Kilner jars
page 17

Stencilled storage crate
page 170

Appliquéd & embroidered rose tea towel
page 32

Blackbird cross-stitch tea towel
page 31

Colour key

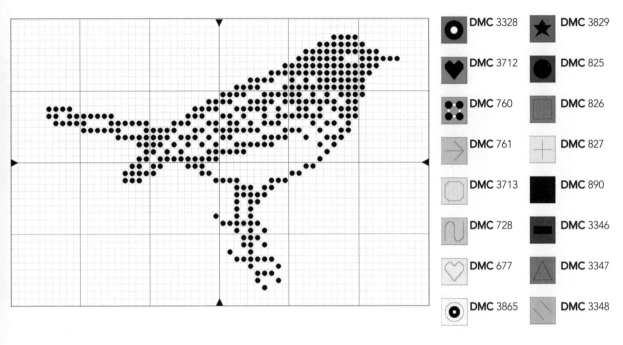

◉	DMC 3328	★	DMC 3829
♥	DMC 3712	●	DMC 825
⠿	DMC 760	▢	DMC 826
→	DMC 761	+	DMC 827
▢	DMC 3713	■	DMC 890
∿	DMC 728	▬	DMC 3346
♡	DMC 677	△	DMC 3347
◉	DMC 3865	╲	DMC 3348

Upcycled gypsy rose footstool
page 71

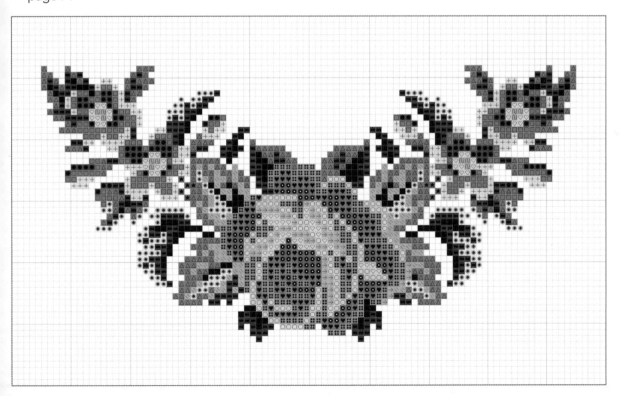

Pressed flowers calendar
page 88

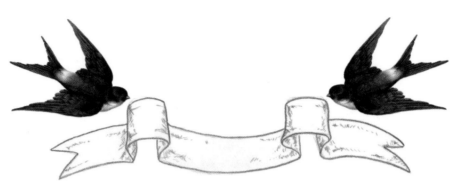

Monday	Tuesday	Wednesday	Thursday	Friday	Saturday	Sunday

Lace Christmas stockings
page 94

Lace Christmas crackers
page 97

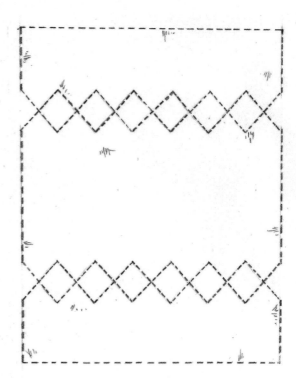

Butterfly bed linen
page 113

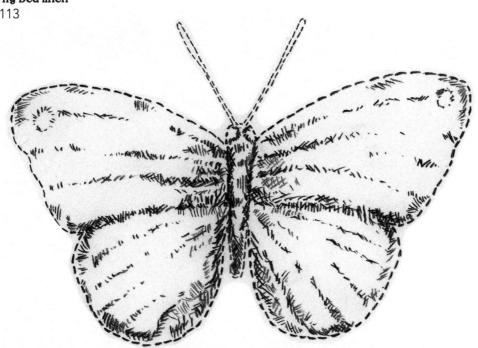

Vinyl ceiling rose
page 140

Bird wall stickers
page 141

Lavender & lace heart
page 133

Decorative china plates
page 164

Screen-printed floral wallpaper
page 174
(roses and leaves to be traced separately)

Index

Thank you

This book is dedicated to my husband Danny and my four wonderful children: Daisy, Alfie, Frankie and Betty, for not only being a constant source of inspiration, but for also putting up with all our many house moves. I knew one day there would be a reason for it all!

Thanks also to my mum and dad for being so supportive; to Elaine, Adam, Cheryl and their gorgeous families; to Linda, Chris, Nic, Cazza, Ed, Gita, Rhys, Patsy, Lisa, Victoria, Georgia, Heidi, Alicia, Caroline, Frances, Catherine, Cathy, Flavia, Marguerite, Anita, Nicola, Katie and all my lovely Somerset friends – thanks for bringing joy into my life. And thanks to Zoe, for being the bestest friend anyone could ever wish for. And to Abbey, for sharing my vision and never letting me give up, for all your wonderful illustrations, words and ideas. Without you, this book wouldn't have been possible.

Thanks to my editor, Elen Jones, and to Lizzy Gray and Georgina Atsiaris; to Martin Topping and Lucy Sykes-Thompson for the beautiful design; and all at HarperCollins for believing in this book as much as me. To Helena Caldon and Emma Callery who helped write and carefully edit the book; to Debi Treloar and Marianne Cotterill for the beautiful photography; to Diana Moar, Julie Jacobs and Megumi Matsuno who styled my hair and make-up. Thanks to Carol Hayes and Karin Silverstein at Carol Hayes Management; Neil Blair, Zoe King, Daniel Teweles and everyone at The Blair Partnership; and Melvyn du Bell for sorting out my finances.

Thanks also to Yvonne Williams for your guidance; to Jo Weinberg, for the delicious food; Susie Bell for the insanely real flowers; to Faye Chadburn for the creations on our gypsy wagon; it's perfection! To Mim for helping me find the words; to Jaywood in Frome, thank you for helping us create wonderful spaces in all our houses; to Jo at the Walled Garden at Mells; Bramble and Wild and The Blossom Tree for supplying all the lovely plants and flowers; to Lisa for your invaluable help around the house. Thanks also to Howie & Belle and Scarlet & Violet for letting us shoot in their lovely shops; to Foxy Brown's Cakes and Bakes and the Primrose Bakery for the delicious treats; to Oh Sew Helena, What Delilah Did and Jessica Lennox for their crafty advice; to Brigette and Robin from Odd Limited for lending all the tribal rugs and cushions; to Rachel Ashwell for lending her cushions, napkins and rugs; to Annie Sloan for the paint; GF Smith for the paper; James Hare for the lace and silk; and House of Hackney and Mel at Wallpaper Direct for all the fantastic wallpaper. Thanks also to Vicky Trainor, Spotted Sparrow, Frou Frou and Thomas, Lauren Moriarty, Nostalgia at the Stone House, Susannah Decorative Antiques and Textiles, Sharp and Noble, Darby & Joan, Betty Bee Vintage, British Cream Tea and Supernice.

First published in 2013 by Collins
HarperCollinsPublishers
77–85 Fulham Palace Road
London W6 8JB

www.harpercollins.co.uk

10 9 8 7 6 5 4 3 2 1

Text © Pearl Lowe 2013
Photography © Debi Treloar 2013

Pearl Lowe asserts her moral right to be identified as the author of this work

A catalogue record for this book is available from the British Library

ISBN: 978-0-00-749109-4

Styling: Marianne Cotterill
Illustrations: Abigail Warner
Edit: Emma Callery
Additional text: Helena Caldon

Printed and bound in China by R R Donnelley

All rights reserved. No parts of this publication may be reproduced, stored in a retrieval system or transmitted, in any form or by any means, electronic, mechanical, photocopying, recording or otherwise, without the prior permission of the publishers.

Disclaimer The publisher and the author have made every reasonable effort to ensure that the projects and activities in this book are safe when carried out as instructed but assume no responsibility for any damage caused or sustained while undertaking the projects or activities in this book to the full extent permitted by law. This book is intended for adults only as some of the processes and materials used could result in injury or harm if not used in accordance with the proper instructions. Any parents choosing to allow their children to assist must ensure that they are fully supervised at all times.

WARNING/SAFETY INSTRUCTIONS
ALWAYS follow all the steps in each project carefully.
TAKE CARE, especially when handling hot or heavy objects, glass, scissors, knives, matches, candles, corrosive materials or other potentially dangerous materials.
ALWAYS read the safety instructions on any products and materials used and ensure that you follow the manufacturer's guidelines and take all appropriate safety precautions.

Collins